SURA'S

SCHOOL
ENGLISH
GRAMMAR

By
Prof. Y. Krishna Murthy, M.A., M.Phil., (Retd.)

SURA COLLEGE OF COMPETITION
Chennai ● Bangalore ● Kolkata

Price: Rs.35.00

© **PUBLISHERS**

School English Grammar

Price: Rs.35.00

ISBN: 81-7254-161-9

Sura College of Competition

o   1620, 'J' Block,
     16th Main Road,
     Anna Nagar,
     Chennai - 600 040.
     Phones: 91-44-6162173, 6162924

Printed at **Chennai Micro Print (P) Ltd.,** Chennai - 600 029 and Published
by **V.V.K.Subburaj** for **Sura College of Competition,** 1620, 'J' Block,
16th Main Road, Anna Nagar, Chennai - 600 040. Phones: 91-44-6162173,
6162924. Fax: (91) 44-6162173. email: surabooks@eth.net

PREFACE

A number of grammar books are written in order to educate the students of English Language and Literature. But those texts contain either too much of material that cannot be made use of by the students or too little of information that is exactly required by the students. Taking into consideration, the need of the modern student who wants a workable knowledge of English and at the same time quite enough for his further reading and improvement, this book has been designed and executed.

This book contains all the most important aspects of grammar from the fundamental principles like the parts of speech, etc. Modern students' knowledge of the fundamentals of English Grammar leaves much to be desired. Special importance has been given to usage of tenses, voices in the verbs. Forms of sentences, i.e., simple, complex and compound sentences are dealt with in detail along with interchange of complex, simple and compound sentences. Common errors, antonyms, synonyms are also included.

In Composition, all important aspects have been explained from Paraphrasing to Report and Paragraph Writing. Exercises have been included for training the students. Care has been taken to see that the text does not become voluminous. A sincere and precise attempt is made to make grammar as simple and understandable as possible. I hope this grammar book will be of very good use to any high school and college student.

Y. KRISHNA MURTHY
Author

CONTENTS

CHAPTER		Page No.

PART 1

GRAMMAR

CHAPTER I
PARTS OF SPEECH

LANGUAGE is the medium of expression or communication. Every language has it's finer points and peculiarities. Language is of two kinds namely Spoken Language and Written Language. While spoken language is important, it has its own limitations. But Written Language is of far reaching importance. It is permanent and reaches every nook and corner of the globe. Written language is responsible for the rise and growth of literature and its various ramifications.

It is when we come to written language that we think of principles of grammar and composition. Any study of language cannot be called complete or comprehensive unless the words, the chief components are mastered in their usage and placement. Thus arises the importance of Parts of Speech in the English language.

There are **eight** parts of speech in the English language. Each part of speech a definite and distinctive function to perform. It is only the combination of these parts of speech that gives us the meaning of what others want to convey to us.

The eight parts of speech in the English Language are:

i.	Noun	ii.	Pronoun
iii.	Verb	iv.	Adverb
v.	Adjective	vi.	Preposition
vii.	Interjection	viii.	Conjunction

1

All words in English language fall into these eight divisions. Hence a proper understanding of these parts of speech, their functions, qualities and usages are absolutely essential for the mastery of the language. Let us see the various parts of speech by defining them and citing examples.

i.   A NOUN is the name of a person, place, animal or thing.

e.g.:   Rama, Krishna, London, Jimmy, Pilot, dog, bench, town, boy etc.

ii. A PRONOUN is a word used instead of a noun.

e.g.:   I, we, you, he, she, it, they etc.

iii. A VERB is a word which denotes the action of the subject.

e.g.:   The sun **rises** in the east.
She **sang** a song.
Boys are **playing** foot ball.

iv. An ADVERB is a word which modifies a verb, adjective or other adverb. Sometimes they qualify even prepositions and conjunctions.

e.g.:   He ran **fast.** They came **quickly.**
There he remained. etc.

v.   An ADJECTIVE is a word which qualifies a noun or pronoun. It adds something to the meaning.

e.g.:   **beautiful** face, **sparkling** eyes,
dancing girl

vi. A PREPOSITION is a word placed before a noun or pronoun to make complete sense.

e.g.:   in, on, of, at, upon, under, above, below etc.

2

vii. An INTERJECTION is a word expressing an emotion - fear, shock, pity, wonder, sorrow, joy etc.

    e.g.: Alas! Ah! Hurrah! Lo! etc.

viii. A CONJUNCTION is a word that joins two words or sentences.

    e.g.: and, but, or etc.

EXERCISE

1. How many parts of speech are there in English?

2. Write the various parts of speech with examples?

3. Define Verb and Preposition with examples.

4. What are Interjections and Conjunctions? Illustrate.

CHAPTER II
KINDS OF NOUNS

NOUNS are generally classified under **five** heads. They are:

i. PROPER NOUNS denoting particular names of persons, places, animals and things.

e.g.: Rama, Delhi, Swan (Pen), Jimmy (Dog)

ii. COMMON NOUNS denoting general names of persons, places, animals and things.

e.g.: boy, city, pen, dog etc.

iii. COLLECTIVE NOUNS denoting in one word a collection of many persons, animals and things.

e.g.: bunch, fleet, flock, herd, galaxy, constellation, crowd, army, bevy, etc.

iv. MATERIAL NOUNS denoting a material out of which other materials are made.

e.g.: gold, silver, zinc, mud, clay, plastic etc.

v. ABSTRACT NOUNS denoting the name of a quality, state or action.

e.g.: knowledge, wisdom, courage, bravery, childhood etc.

Every NOUN and PRONOUN have the following **four** qualities.

i. Kind

ii. Number

iii. Gender

iv. Case

We have seen the kinds of noun already.

ii. A NOUN or PRONOUN is singular when it refers to one person, animal, place or thing. It is plural when it denotes more than one person, place, animal or thing.

e.g.:	Singular	Plural
	man	men
	child	children
	I	We
	Pen	Pens
	He	They

Generally plural is formed by the addition of **s** or **es** to the singular. (Sometimes with a change of the final letter i.e. f to v, y to i).

(e.g.: -f to -v, -y to i)

	Singular	Plural
	Boy	Boys
	Ass	Asses
	Calf	Calves
	Fly	Flies

Some words form the plural by the addition of **en** to the singular.

e.g.:	ox	-	oxen
	child	-	children

5

Some words get changed by vowel.

e.g.:   mouse - mice

                goose - geese

Some words have the same form in singular and plural.

Singular	Plural
Sheep	Sheep
Swine	Swine

Greek Words:

analysis	analyses
phenomenon	phenomena

Latin Words:

Axis	Axes
Fungus	Fungi
Genius	Genii (spirits)
	Geniuses
Index	Indices
Memorandum	Memoranda
Stratum	Strata

Hebrew Words:

Cherub	Cherubim
Seraph	Seraphim

Compound words form their plural by adding **s** to the chief word.

e.g.:		
	Father-in-law	Fathers-in-law
	Step son	Step sons
	Hanger on	Hangers on

6

Passer by	Passers by
Court martial	Courts martial

iii. There are FOUR GENDERS in NOUNS. They are (1) Masculine (all male objects & persons) (2) Feminine (all female objects & persons) (3) Common (either male or female) (4) Neuter (neither male nor female).

e.g.:

Masculine	Feminine
Horse	Mare
Dog	Bitch
Man	Woman
Boy	Girl
Master	Mistress

Common Gender:

e.g.: Doctor, Nurse, Teacher, Lawyer, Servant, etc.

Neuter Gender:

e.g.: Table, Chair, Desk, Book, etc.,

iv. CASE ending in nouns denotes its relationship to the other words in the sentence. There are **four** important cases.

1. The subject of the sentence is said to be in the NOMINATIVE CASE.

e.g.: I gave the book to my friend.

'I' is in the nominative case as it is the subject in the sentence.

2. The object of the sentence is said to be in the OBJECTIVE or ACCUSATIVE CASE..

2

'Book' is in the accusative case as it is the object in the sentence.

3. VOCATIVE case is used to address a person or thing.

   e.g.: Sir! What do you mean?

4. The GENETIVE or POSSESSIVE case indicates the owner or possessor.

   e.g.: boy's hat, student's book, whose hat is that? etc.

EXERCISE

1. How many kinds of nouns are there? What are they? Give examples.

2. How do you form plurals in nouns? Give examples.

3. What are Genders? How many are there for nouns? Give examples.

4. Give the names of cases in nouns and explain with examples.

CHAPTER III
KINDS OF PRONOUNS

PRONOUNS are divided into the following kinds.

a. PERSONAL PRONOUNS

These are further classified into First Person (Person Speaking)

e.g.: I, We

Second Person (Person Spoken to)

e.g.: you

Third Person

e.g.: He, She, it, they, them, him, her, etc.

b. POSSESSIVE PRONOUNS indicating proprietary rights.

e.g.: mine, ours, yours, his, hers, its, theirs etc.

c. EMPHATIC PRONOUNS to show emphasis

e.g.: The King **himself** was present.

d. REFLEXIVE PRONOUNS denote the samething or person as the subject and are placed in the object position.

e.g.: He did the job for **himself**

e. DEMONSTRATIVE PRONOUNS denote the person or thing to which they refer.

e.g.: this, that, these, those, such, some, etc.

9

f. INTERROGATIVE PRONOUNS are used in asking questions.

e.g.: Who, Whom, Whose, Which, What, etc.

g. RELATIVE PRONOUNS are related to a Noun or Pronoun which generally precedes it. This noun or pronoun before a relative pronoun is called the antecedent.

e.g.: who, whom, whose, which, that, what and sometimes as and but. **Who** is used for persons.

Which and **What** indicate things.

e.g.: This is the **house that** Ramu built.

That is the relative pronoun.
House is the antecedent.

A RELATIVE PRONOUN acts both as a conjunction joining two clauses and as a subject, object or after a preposition.

Whoever, Whatsoever are special forms of RELATIVES without antecedents.

As is a relative Pronoun after the words such same.

e.g.: His answer is the same **as** his mother gave.

But is a relative pronoun after a negative.

e.g.: There is no one **but** hates him.

A relative pronoun may be omitted if it is the object of the verb following it.

e.g.: Did I tell you about the strong man (whom) I saw yesterday?

A relative pronoun cannot be omitted if it is the subject of its clause.

e.g.: The man who was run over has been h o s p i - t a l i z e d.

h. NUMERAL PRONOUNS indicate numbers .

e.g.: one, two, three etc.

i. INDEFINITIVE PRONOUNS denote a vague number or amount .

e.g.:

any	more
neither	all
many	anybody
each	little
something	few
enough	everyone
much	either.

CHAPTER IV
KINDS OF ADJECTIVES AND ADVERBS

AN adjective is always used with a noun. In other words it qualifies a noun or pronoun.

The following are the main divisions in ADJECTIVES.

a. DESCRIPTIVE ADJECTIVES describe a person or thing (usually a quality)

e.g.: good, beautiful, evil, useful.

b. POSSESSIVE ADJECTIVES indicate the ownership of the article or thing.

e.g.: my, our, your, his, her, its, their

Pronoun	Adjective
This is **mine**	This is **my** book.
Is that **yours?**	I have found **my** box.
He said it was **his**.	Have you seen **his** bag.

c. EMPHATIC ADJECTIVES denote a strong stress and affirmation.

e.g.: I am my **own** master.
The **very** dogs hate him.

d. DEMONSTRATIVE ADJECTIVES point out to certain persons and things.

e.g.: this, that, these, those, such, same etc.
He came to **this** city.
What are **those** questions?

'The' is a demonstrative adjective and is called the Definite Article.

e. INTERROGATIVE ADJECTIVES ask questions.

e.g.: **What** reply did you give?
Which way did he take?

f. RELATIVE ADJECTIVES are used with nouns to introduce relative clauses.

e.g.: Take **which** present you prefer.
He used **what** material he had.

g. NUMERAL ADJECTIVES are used to denote numbers.

i. Cardinal Numerals.

e.g.: **one** boy; **three** men.

ii. Ordinal numerals show the position in a series.

e.g.: First **place**, Second **place**, etc.

h. INDEFINITE ADJECTIVES are similar to Indefinite Pronouns and can be used like them

e.g.: **Few** people were present.
Other friends objected
Each man has his own problem
Some cats have no tails.

ADVERBS

ADVERBS generally fall into the following sub divisions:

a. SIMPLE ADVERBS denoting time, place, manner, number, reason, degree etc.

e.g.: He came **soon**.
I have **never** seen him **so** angry.
Therefore he came out successful.

13

b. INTERROGATIVE ADVERBS ask questions.

> *e.g.:* **Where** did you meet him?
> **When** will he return?
> **How** are you?
> **Why** do you think like that?

RELATIVE ADVERBS are similar to relative pronouns as they relate to antecedent and also connect two clauses.

> *e.g.:* This is the town **where** he lived.
> Tell me the reason **why** you are sad.
> Summer is the time **when** people move out to hill stations.

ADJECTIVES and ADVERBS are very often used in comparing one person or thing to others. There are three degrees of comparison (1) POSITIVE (2) COMPARATIVE and (3) SUPERLATIVE.

The comparative is generally formed by adding **er** to the positive and the superlative by adding **est** to the positive. In cases where there are more than one syllable 'more' is added in the comparative and 'most' in the superlative.

e.g.:	Positive	Comparative	Superlative
	happy	happier	happiest
	sad	sadder	saddest
	beautiful	more beautiful	most beautiful
	well	better	best
	far	farther	farthest

CHAPTER V
PREPOSITIONS, INTERJECTIONS AND CONJUNCTIONS

THE PREPOSITION means 'a word placed before'.

PREPOSITION, therefore, is a word placed before a noun or pronoun to make complete sense. It shows the relationship of the thing or person to something else.

> e.g.: He is fond **of** tea.
> The cat jumped **off** the chair.

KINDS OF PREPOSITIONS

1. SIMPLE PREPOSITIONS are used for large countries and towns, to speak of things at rest, in motion, of time, place, to indicate instrument, agent etc.

> e.g.: He lives **in** America.
> My friend lives **at** Saidapet **in** Madras.
> Ramu is **in** bed
> John is **at** the top of the class.
> He jumped **into** the well.
> I ran **to** him.
> They sat **on** the cot.
> The dog sprang **upon** the table.
> Shyam **slept** till 8 o'clock.
> They came **to** the end of the street.
> He killed two birds **with** one shot.
> He was stabbed **by** a stranger.
> **Beside** (by the side of) the man stood the child.

Besides (in addition to) medals he won a number of cups also.

2. COMPOUND PREPOSITIONS are formed by prefixing to a noun, an adjective or adverb.

   e.g.: about   above   behind
            across   along   below
            among   before   beneath
            beside   between etc.

   He is the best **among** my friends.
   The bridge is **across** the river.

3. PHRASE PREPOSITIONS or PREPOSITIONAL PHRASES are prepositions added on to verbs and give the force of a single preposition.

   e.g.: according to   in addition to
            because of   by means of
            in order to   etc.

   I will act **according to** your wish.
   In addition to his knowledge, he has wisdom too.
   Because of rain the match was cancelled.
   By means of his help she could come out without harm.
   In order to win one has to work hard.

4. PARTICIPLE PREPOSITIONS are those present participles of verbs used absolutely without any noun or pronoun.

   e.g.: Barring,   during,   notwithstanding,
          pending,   regarding, considering etc.

   A preposition is said to govern a noun or pronoun that follows it.

Most prepositions may be used as adverbs also. The test for a preposition is that it is always followed by a noun or pronoun. This quality is useful in distinguishing it from an adverb.

e.g.:	**ADVERB**	**PREPOSITION**
	He walked **by**	He walked **by** the river.
	I looked **up**	I looked **up** the street.
	He remained **behind**	He remained **behind** the tree

INTERJECTIONS denote any kind of emotion. They have no other part in grammar except to indicate the various shades of feelings like joy and sorrow, surprise and shock, wonder and admiration, pity or a wish. They are mostly followed by exclamations.

> *e.g.:* alas! Ah! oh! Hurrah! Lo! behold! etc.

CONJUNCTIONS are words joining two words or sentences. Generally they are divided into two kinds. COORDINATING CONJUNCTIONS connect words or phrases or clauses of equal position and are, therefore independent of one another.

> *e.g.:* He **and** I cannot come together (connecting words).
> The man is always to be found in the library **or** in the garden (phrases).
> I argued with him **but** he disagreed (connecting coordinating clauses)

Examples of other coordinating conjunctions: still, yet, so, for, therefore.

A few pairs of words serve as coordinating conjunctions. They are called correlative conjunctions.

e.g.: both · · · · · · · · and
      either · · · · · · · or
      not only · · · · · but also etc.

SUBORDINATING CONJUNCTIONS join the noun or adverb clauses to main clause. Some of the most common subordinating conjunctions are

that	unless
when	how
since	though
after	because
if	as
than	why

EXERCISE

1. Define Preposition.

2. Give a list of different kinds of Prepositions with examples.

3. How do you differentiate an adverb from a preposition? Explain with examples.

4. What are the types of conjunction? Give examples and explain.

CHAPTER VI
THE VERB

VERB can be defined as a word that denotes the action of the subject.

Verbs are divided into **three** main classes.

a. A TRANSITIVE VERB indicates an action that directly passes on to the object.

e.g.: He built the house.

In other words Transitive Verbs are those that have objects.
In change of voice only transitive verbs can be changed into the passive voice.

b. INTRANSITIVE VERBS are those whose action does not pass on to the object. In other words intransitive verbs do not have objects. A number of verbs may be transitive or intransitive according to the sentence in which they are used.

e.g.: He **strikes** the ball (Transitive)
The clock **strikes** (Intransitive)
Ring the bell (Transitive)
The bell **rings** (Intransitive)

An Intransitive verb some times takes a cognate object (closely connected in meaning)

e.g.: He ran (a race) - cognate object.
I have lived (my life) - cognate object.

c. An AUXILIARY VERB is not used alone but helps another verb to form a voice, tense or mood.

> *e.g.:* I **am** driven.
> I **shall** inform.
> You **may** go.

The Auxiliary verbs are Be, Have, Do, May, Shall, Will.

Some intransitive verbs do not make sense without a predicative adjective or noun or noun equivalent.

> *e.g.:* She seems **ill**.
> She soon became **angry**.
> This is **What I foresaw**.

Such verbs which cannot have a complete predicate are called VERBS OF INCOMPLETE PREDICATION.

> *e.g.:* be, seem, become, be made, be supposed,
> be called, be named.

A few transitive verbs are incapable of giving complete sense without a predicative word. Thus they are also verbs of Incomplete Predication.

> *e.g.:* Parliament **made** the member as the chairman.
> The drink **made** him ill.
> The doctor **pronounced** him dead.

In addition to the three main classes of verbs, a few verbs like strong, weak and finite verbs exist.

STRONG VERBS are those that change their spelling and sound in the past tense.

> *e.g.:* teach   taught
> catch   caught etc.

WEAK VERBS form their past tense by the addition of **ed**, **d** or **t** to the present form.

e.g.: Present Tense	Past Tense	Past Participle
look	looked	looked
fear	feared	feared
spend	spent	spent

FINITE VERBS are always limited by the person and number of the subject in the sentence.

e.g.: He goes.

Here the subject 'he' and the verb 'goes' are in third person singular number.

Verbs in their basic forms expressing simply the notion of the verb without any object are called the INFINITIVES.

e.g.: to love, to hate, to be, to see, etc.

Verbs have a special quality denoted as VOICE. Voice points out whether a subject in the sentence acts by itself or is acted upon.

Thus there are two voices for all transitive verbs. They are :
1. **Active Voice**
2. **Passive Voice**

The most important and useful quality of verb is its TENSE.

By these tenses we denote the time of action, the continuance of action and also the completeness of the action.

All verbs are grouped under THREE MOODS - the IN-DICATIVE, the IMPERATIVE and the SUBJUNCTIVE.

a. INDICATIVE MOOD generally denotes statements and interrogations

e.g.: He will come immediately.
Did you attend?

b. IMPERATIVE MOOD is used for commands or entreaties (requests) in the second person only.

e.g.: Shut the door
Forgive him.

c. THE SUBJUNCTIVE MOOD is almost extinct in modern English. The subjunctive mood is used to show something that is thought of as being desirable or likely to happen.

e.g.: God save the King.
I wish I were you.
They wondered if he were the culprit.
If that were so I should be annoyed.

The following verbs with an infinitive without, to are used as subjunctive equivalents.

e.g.: may, might, shall, should, would.
May you be happy after all your sorrows.

EXERCISE

1. What is a verb?
2. What are the kinds of verbs? Give examples.
3. What is Voice? How many are there? Give examples.
4. What are the different moods of the verb? Explain with examples.

CHAPTER VII
USAGE OF TENSES

THERE are **three** main TENSES in English.

They are   **(1) Present Tense**
            (2) Past Tense
            (3) Future Tense

PRESENT TENSE indicates action taking place in the present - at the time of speaking.

PAST TENSE shows an action that has taken place already in the past.

FUTURE TENSE indicates any action likely to take place at a later date - in future.

Each main tense viz., PRESENT, PAST, FUTURE is divided into four subdivisions to facilitate proper expression of the time of action, its continuance or completeness. Thus instead of generally describing an action it is easy to pinpoint the time of action, its continuance and completion either in the present, past or future.

The four subdivisions are :
PRESENT

1. Simple Present Tense
2. Present Continuous Tense
3. Present Perfect Tense
4. Present Perfect Continuous Tense

23

PAST

5. Simple Past Tense

6. Past Continuous Tense

7. Past Perfect Tense

8. Past Perfect Continuous Tense

FUTURE

9. Simple Future Tense

10. Future Continuous Tense

11. Future Perfect Tense

12. Future Perfect Continuous Tense

It is absolutely essential for any student of English Language to know and master the usages of these tenses in order to express his ideas in relation to time, continuance and completeness.

1. SIMPLE PRESENT TENSE is used to describe daily actions, customs and habits, routine work, proverbs etc. It is also used to give future meaning.

> e.g.:   I **walk** to college daily.
> He **takes** coffee at 8 A.M. every day.
> Usually he **visits** the park in the evening.
> Two and two **makes** four.
> He **comes** tomorrow.
> The sun **rises** in the east.

2. PRESENT CONTINUOUS TENSE is formed by adding **ing to the verb** (verb + ing). It indicates action taking place at the time of speaking but likely to be completed within a reasonable time.

> *e.g.:*   Sita **is singing** a song.
> Boys **are playing** foot ball.
> Students **are doing** exercises.
> I am **reading** the newspaper.

The form 'going to' is used sometimes to indicate future meaning.

> *e.g.:*   My friend is **going to** come tomorrow.

3. PRESENT PERFECT TENSE indicates any action completed in the present - immediate present.

The verbal form is **has + Past Participle** in the singular number and **have + Past Participle** in the plural number.

> *e.g.:*   He **has done** the job.
> She **has finished** her work at home.
> They **have seen** the exhibition.

In these sentences present perfect tense indicates that the action is completed but that not much time has elapsed from the time of speaking.

4. Present Perfect Continuous Tense is generally used to indicate action that had taken place long back and continue in the present and likely to continue further in the future. The verbal forms are

> **Singular** :   **has been + verb + ing**
> **Plural**   :   **have been + verb + ing**
>
> *e.g.:*   He **has been waiting** at the bus stop since evening.
> I **have been residing** at Madras since 1940 onwards.
> The child **has been crying** since morning.

25

5. SIMPLE PAST TENSE is used for all actions in the past irrespective of the point of time. Like the simple present it is used for daily actions and routine work in the past.

> *e.g.:* I **used to walk** daily to the college last year.
> She **sang** daily in the evenings at the temple last week.

6. PAST CONTINUOUS TENSE is used for all actions in the past but not completed at the time of speaking.

The verbal form is past form of the verb + ing.

Singular : **was + verb +ing**
Plural : **were + verb + ing**

> *e.g.:* Sita **was singing** a song.
> Pilgrims **were going** round the Taj Mahal.
> Teachers **were valuing** answer scripts.

Past Continuous is also used to show the exact time of some action taking place.

> *e.g.:* When I **was reading** the novel the lights went off suddenly.

(Continuous Tense shows pointedly the time of the failure of lights).

7. PAST PERFECT TENSE shows actions completed distinctly in the past. It also indicates the particular time - earlier or later - when two actions are described in a sentence.

The verbal form, both in the singular and plural is **had + Past Participle.**

> *e.g.:* I **had seen** him earlier.
> They **had visited** the library many times.

26

The train **had** already **left** the platform when we reached the station (train's departure is earlier).

8. PAST PERFECT CONTINUOUS TENSE like the present perfect continuous is used for long standing actions in the past.

The verbal form is **had been + verb + ing**.

e.g.: He **had been reading** the novel for six months.

9. SIMPLE FUTURE TENSE indicates action likely to take place at some time after the present.

e.g.: He **will come** in a week.
They **shall follow** my instructions tomorrow.

10. FUTURE CONTINUOUS TENSE indicates an action continuing at a point of time in future.

Verbal form : **shall or will be + verb + ing**

e.g.: Sita **will be singing** at the temple this time next week.
They **will be writing** their examinations this day next month.

11. FUTURE PERFECT TENSE indicates completion of action in the future verbal form {shall,will} **+ have + Past Participle.**

e.g.: He **will have finished** writing his papers by this time tomorrow.
By the time I reach Madras they **will have left** for Bombay.

12. FUTURE PERFECT CONTINUOUS TENSE is not used in Modern English generally.

CHAPTER VIII
ACTIVE AND PASSIVE VOICE

$\mathbf{A}$ verb in a sentence is in ACTIVE VOICE if the subject is ACTIVE.

>   e.g.:   Sita **sang** a song.

In this sentence Sita the subject of the verb sang is active. Therefore the verb is in the active voice.

If the subject is not active or if it is passive then the verb is PASSIVE.

>   e.g.:   A song **was sung** by sita.

Here the subject song is not active. So the voice is passive.

Only transitive verbs can be changed into passive voice and vice versa.

*   Rules for change of active voice into Passive Voice.

1.   The SUBJECT in the active voice becomes the OBJECT in the Passive Voice.

2.   The OBJECT in the active voice becomes the SUBJECT in the Passive Voice.

3.   The meaning of the sentence does not change in the other voice.

4.   The TENSE of the verb also does not change.

5. Preposition 'by' is used in the passive voice to give complete sense to the sentence.

Care must be taken to change the voice without changing the tense of the verbs given and taking into consideration singular and plural subjects and objects.

A few examples are given below:

1. Boys are learning grammar (Active)
   Grammar is being learnt by boys (Passive)

2. James ate many cakes (Active)
   Many cakes were eaten by James (Passive)

3. He will finish the job in a fortnight (Active)
   The job will be finished by him in a fortnight (Passive)

The following are examples of ACTIVE and PASSIVE Voice according to the various TENSE FORMATIONS.

1. **SIMPLE PRESENT**

   a. He **sees** the picture. (Active)
      The picture **is seen** by him. (Passive)

   b. John **eats** many cakes (Active)
      Many cakes **are eaten** by James (Passive)

2. **PRESENT CONTINUOUS**

   a. Sita **is singing** a song (Active)

   b. A song is **being sung** by sita (Passive)

In changing continuous tense into passive voice the word 'being' is used after the main verb and before the past participle.

3. **PRESENT PERFECT**

   has + Past Participle   (Active Voice)
   have + Past Participle (Active Voice)

has been + Past Participle   (Passive Voice)
have been + Past Participle (Passive Voice)

a. He **has done** the job (Active)
His job **has been done** by him (Passive)

b. They **have seen** the exhibition (Active)
The exhibition **has been seen** by them (Passive)

c. He **has written** many letters (Active)
Many letters **have been written** by him (Passive)

4. SIMPLE PAST TENSE

a. He **finished** his job (Active)
His job **was finished** by him. (Passive)

b. They **ate** many mangoes (Active)
Many mangoes **were eaten** by them (Passive)

5. PAST CONTINUOUS TENSE

was + verb + ing   (Active)
were + verb + ing (Active)

was + being + verb + ing   (Passive)
were + being + verb + ing (Passive)

a. They **were playing** football (Active)
Foot ball **was being played** by them (Passive)

b. He was **working out** exercises (Active)
Exercises **were being worked out** by him (Passive)

6. PAST PERFECT TENSE

had + past participle (singular & plural) (Active)
had been + past participle (singular & plural) (Passive)

a. They **had done** the job. (Active)
They job **had been done** by them (Passive)

b. People **had seen** the sights (Active)
The sights **had been seen** by the people.

7. **SIMPLE FUTURE TENSE**

Shall or will + verb (Active)
Shall or will + be + Past Participle.(Passive Voice)

a. She **shall sing** a song (Active)
A song **shall be sung** by her (Passive)

b. They will **surely win** the election (Active)
The election **will surely be won** by them (Passive)

8. **FUTURE CONTINUOUS**

Shall/will + be + verb + ing (Active)
Shall/will + be + being + Past Participle (Passive)

e.g.: He **will be finishing** the job soon.
The job **will be being finished** soon.

9. **FUTURE PERFECT TENSE**

will/shall + have + Past Participle (Active)
will/shall + have + been + Past Participle (Passive)

a. They **will have finished** the work by then (Active)
The work **will have been finished** by them then
(Passive)

When there are two objects for the verb two
sentences are formed in the passive voice.

e.g. He gave me money (Active)
Here there are two objects viz. 'money' and 'me'.
Therefore in passive voice, we can form two sentences.

I was given money by him (Passive)
Money **was given** to me (by him) (Passive)

In some cases, in prepositional phrases the word 'by' is not used in the passive voice.

> e.g.: Your **conduct** surprises me (Active)
> I am **surprised at** your conduct (Passive)

('to be surprised at' is a Prepositional Phrase)

Some times the prepositional phrase is used along with the word 'by' in the passive voice.

> e.g.: The old man **looks after** the house. (Active)
> The house **is looked after** by the old man (Passive)

INTERROGATIVE SENTENCES are changed to passive voice similarly.

> e.g.: Who **wrote** this letter? (Active)
> By whom **was this letter written**? (Passive)
> **Did you** post those letters? (Active)
> **Were those letters posted** by you? (Passive)

IMPERATIVE SENTENCES follow a different pattern in the passive voice.

> e.g.: **Shut** the door (Active)
> Let the door **be shut** (by you) (Passive)

'You' is the subject in the active voice but it is understood. Hence 'by you' in passive voice need not be written.

> e.g.: Please **get** me a cup of water (Active)
> Let a cup of water **be got** for me (Passive)

Words of request or politeness like 'please' are omitted in Passive Voice.

In changing the voice of INFINITIVES there is a different pattern.

a. I want him **to do** the job (Active)
I want the job **to be done** by him (Passive)

b. I wish you **to visit** the exhibition (Active)
I wish the exhibition **to be visited** by you (Passive)

Gerunds are changed into passive voice on the model of present continuous tense with the ending **ing**.

e.g.: I like **reading** Novels (Active)
I like novels **being read** (Passive)
They love **visiting** exhibitions (Active)
They love exhibitions **being visited** (Passive)

EXERCISE

Change the Voice of the Verb:

1. The cat killed the mouse.
2. He eats mangoes.
3. She has done the job.
4. Boys are playing foot ball.
5. They have seen the picture.
6. The job has been done by him.
7. She was bitten by a dog.
8. I want you to do the job.
9. He gave me money.
10. Raju laughed at him.

CHAPTER IX
INFINITIVES, GERUNDS AND PARTICIPLES

INFINTIVES are otherwise called as Verbal Nouns as they are used both as verbs and nouns.

In the same manner Gerunds are also called verbal nouns. Both the infinitive and gerund are used as subject and object of the sentence. While all Infinitives have 'to' along with the verb the gerund has the ing ending.

> *e.g.:* to see (Inf)   to run, to sleep,
> seeing (Ger) running sleeping.

Participles are otherwise called verbal adjectives as they are used like adjectives qualifying a noun or pronoun.

> *e.g.:* Seeing. Though the gerund and participle have the same form (ending with **ing**) they can be distinguished by their usage very easily.

Gerund and Infinitive as Subject

> *e.g.:* **To run** is to improve the body (Infinitive)
> **Running** improves the body (Gerund)

As Object

a. I like **to do** service (Infinitive)

b. I like **doing** service (Gerund)

1. PREDICATIVELY USED

a. My great ambition is **to become** a lawyer (Infinitive)

34

b. My great ambition is **becoming** a lawyer (Gerund)

Some gerunds are governed by preposition and qualified by adjective.

e.g.: I spend my time **in reading** and **writing** (Preposition)

The class was engaged in **silent reading** (Adjective)

Some verbs have for their objects the Infinitive without 'to'. They are

can	may	shall
do	must	will
dare	need	

As a second object after certain verbs like fear, hear, see, make.

e.g.: I made him **go**
He heard the dog **bark**

The participle acts like a verb and so can have an object and be qualified by an adverb.

e.g.: **Violently shutting** the **gate** he departed.
Adjective Participle Object

Participles are used before a noun

e.g.: a running stream, a dancing girl, a broken seed etc.

2. PREDICATIVELY

The children went out **shouting**.
I heard the thunder **rolling** in the distance.

3. TO INTRODUCE AN ADJECTIVE PHRASE

Seeing the crowd gathering, I crossed the road (Participle phrase qualifies the Pronoun 'I')

The special use of the participle is in the NOMINATIVE ABSOLUTE CONSTRUCTION.

e.g.: **a. All attempts having failed**, we abandoned work for the day.

b. All being well, we will start our venture on Wednesday.

In the above participle phrases there is no grammatical connection with the rest of the sentence. Hence the phrase is said to be 'absolute'. The noun or pronoun in the phrase is in the nominative case.

EXERCISE

1. What are Infinitives and Gerunds?

2. How are they used in general? Give examples.

3. What is a Split Infinitive?

4. How do you differentiate a gerund from a participle?

5. What is Nominative Absolute? Give example.

CHAPTER X
RULES OF CONCORD AND COMMON ERRORS IN GRAMMAR

THE rules of concord or agreement govern the relationship of different parts of a sentence to one another.

A verb agrees with its subject in number and person. This rule is general. There are special applications of this rule as detailed below:

a. two or more subjects take a plural verb.

e.g.: He and I are friends

b. Though two subjects are present, if he total idea is one, the verb is singular.

e.g.: My whole aim and object is to make this clear.

c. When phrases like either ... or, neither.... nor are used with the subjects the verb is singular.

e.g.: **Neither** he **nor** his brother **was** there.
Either you leave **or** suffer punishment.

d. If one of the subjects is in plural the verb is in plural.

e.g.: Neither he nor his **brothers were** there.

e. When the subject has nouns or pronouns in different persons and separated by either... or, neither... nor, the verb agrees with the nearer in person.

37

e.g.: Neither Ramu nor **I am** able to be present.

f. A collective noun (singular) can take a singular or plural verb as per its meaning taken as a singular or plural.

e.g.: A new **government** has been formed (singular). The **committee** were divided in their view. (Plural).

g. Two singular nouns joined by 'and' require a plural verb.

e.g.: John and his mother were there.

h. A singular noun followed by phrase introduced by 'with' or 'as well as' takes a singular verb.

e.g.: The King, **with the whole of his followers was** slain.

i. Two singular nouns joined by 'and' denote the same thing and hence take a singular verb.

e.g.: The King and conqueror arrives.

j. If the definite article is repeated before the second noun it means two different persons and the verb must be plural.

e.g.: The poet and the novelist have arrived. (The poet and the novelist are different persons).

k. Plural nouns indicating a single object have a singular verb.

e.g.: Gullivers Travels is a great novel by Swift.

l. A few nouns in plural form generally take a singular verb esp. names of subjects.

e.g.: **Politics** interests him.

38

Mathematics is his favourite subject.
The latest **news** is awaited.

m. Prepositions and Transitive verbs must be followed by the accusative case.

e.g.: Let you and **I** go together   (wrong)
Let you and **me** go together   (right)

Between you and **I** there is no difference
    (wrong)
Between you and **me** there is no difference
    (right)

Who are you referring to?   (wrong)
To whom are you referring to?   (right)

n. Predicative Pronouns agree in case with the word to which they refer

e.g.: If I were **him** I should not go.   (wrong)
If I were **he** I should not go.   (right)

o. Distributive adjectives and Pronouns like Each, Every, Either, Everybody, Anybody, Nobody, None, etc are followed by verbs, pronouns and adjectives in singular.

e.g.: Each person who comes will have **his** own views (not their own views).
No body will be allowed to express **his** opinion (not their opinion).

Has either of you seen my book?   (not have either)
Every book and magazine **was** in **its** proper place
    (not were, their).

39

Than is used as a conjunction and not a preposition. Sometimes error in the case of the pronoun following 'than' occurs. This can be avoided by completing the clause to which the pronoun belongs.

> e.g.: He has been more successful than 'me'.
> (Incorrect)
> He has been more successful than I (have)
> (Correct)

It is better to remove all doubts by completing the last clause in each sentence as in the following

> e.g.: He likes my brother more than he likes me.
> He likes my brother more than I do.

'Hardly' is always followed by 'when' and 'No sooner' by 'than'. 'But' should not be used in their place.

> e.g.: **Hardly** had I left the place **when** the police came searching.
> **No sooner** had I said the word **than** I knew that I was betrayed.

The Gerund (verb, noun with ing ending) must not be used to show its implied subject unless it is qualified by a possessive adjective.

> e.g.: On attempting to restore the picture ...... etc.
> (Incorrect)
> On our attempting to restore the picture ...... etc.
> (Correct)

When the Gerund is preceded by the word 'the' it must be followed by the word 'of'.

e.g.: **The** careful **recording of** these documents etc.
(Gerund)

THE SPLIT INFINITIVE

Generally care should be taken not to split the Infinitive - that is to separate 'to' from the verb word by inserting an adverb or phrase.

e.g.: I expect you to gently pick up this luggage and
to carefully **carry** it.   (Incorrect)
I expect you **to pick up** this luggage gently
and **to carry** it carefully.   (Correct)

The word other is used after a comparative adjective but not after a superlative.

e.g.: Kalidasa is **greater than** any **other** dramatist.

The Superlative form should not be used while speaking of two persons or things.

e.g.: That bag is the finest of the two (Incorrect)
That bag is finer of the two (Correct)

LIE - LAY

The intransitive verb **'to lie'** is confused with the transitive verb **'to lay'**

e.g.: I **lay** the book on the table.
I **lie** on the cot.

The word 'same' is used wrongly in business English.

e.g.: We got your consignment this morning and
thank you for **same** (Incorrect)
We got your consignment this morning and
thank you for **them**. (Correct)

41

'Same' and 'Such' must be followed by 'as' and not by the relative pronoun 'that'.

> *e.g.:*   This is the **same** fellow **as** we saw yesterday.
> He is not a person of **such** character **as** we supposed.

The uses of 'owing to' and 'due to' are generally misunderstood.

Due is an adjective and so qualifies a noun or pronoun.

> *e.g.:*   'The rent is due'; 'He was due to take his turn'.
> **Due to** unforeseen circumstances, we shall have to leave early. (Incorrect).
> **Owing to** unforeseen circumstances we shall have to leave early (Correct).
>
> The untidy condition of the house was **owing to** the owner's absence. (Incorrect)
> The untidy condition of the house was **due to** the owner's absence (Correct).

In the first sentence **owing to** governs the noun that follows.

Due to is used when it is a predicative adjective after the verb 'to be'.

The pairs of conjunctions like 'either...or' not only ... but also, not ... but, both ... and, neither ... nor, should be placed before the same part of speech or kind of phrase.

> *e.g.:*   This is **not** imagination **but** a hard fact.
> He is anxious **not only** to acquire knowledge **but also** eager to display it.   (Incorrect).

He is **not only** anxious to acquire knowledge **but also** eager to display it. (Correct).

Either the decree was just **or** unjust (Incorrect)
The decree was **either** just **or** unjust (Correct)

Exhausted **both** in strength **and** will (Incorrect)
Exhausted **both** in strength **and** in will (Correct)
or
Exhausted in **both** strength **and** will.

LESS

The adjective less indicates quantity. If number is to be indicated 'fewer' must be used.

e.g.:   less bread   less traffic
          fewer rolls   fewer ears

EXERCISE

Correct the following sentences:

1. A necklace of diamonds presented by the friends of the bride, were among the presents on view.

2. The Marquis with his son now at Oxford were present at the function.

3. The team was now in the field and about to take their places.

4. Who were you talking to just now?

43

5. Such rules do not apply to you and I.

6. Nobody offered to give up their seat to her.

7. Neither of them were prepared for the emergency.

8. People do not save money like they used to.

9. He laid for half an hour unconscious until he was seen by a passing motorist.

10. If such a proposal is made, we would be the first to welcome it.

11. She is the tallest of the two girls.

12. None of these men was there.

13. Hardly had he returned than he was called out again.

14. The ten first pages of the book were missing.

15. The quality of films today are inferior.

16. Each of the two have their advantages.

17. He cannot run as quick as I.

18. Neither his brother nor his sister were able to help him.

19. He decided to quickly leave the house.

20. No sooner had he arrived when he was taken straight upto the stranger.

21. Being the only people there, their presence was most important.

22. Every one must do what they think best.

23. One learns to respect himself in the army.

24. Neither of these books are any good for me.

25. Return it back to me today.

CHAPTER XI
THE SENTENCE

A SENTENCE is a group of words arranged in order to make a complete sense.

There are two main parts of a sentence. They are (1) SUBJECT and (2) PREDICATE:

e.g.: Birds fly.
The house is for rent.
Many people present soon went home.

The first part speaks of a word or group of words about which something is said. This is called as the SUBJECT. In the second part something is said about the subject. This is called the PREDICATE.

KINDS OF SENTENCES

a. A sentence may express a statement. Such sentences are called Affirmative or Assertive sentences.

e.g.: He was a great man.
The King was a lover of art.

b. Sentences which ask questions are called Interrogative sentences.

e.g.: What is your name?
Where is your school?

c. Sentences which express a desire, a com-
mand, a request, an entreaty, a wish are called
Imperative sentences.

e.g.: Shut the door
Stop the noise
Please get me a cup of coffee
Kindly help me
May he succeed in the exam.

d. Sentences which express an exclamation, strong feelings of surprise, fear, sadness, joy, shock, etc.

e.g.: How brave he was!
What a lofty idea!
Alas! the bad day!

e. A question but not expecting an answer. The answer is implied within the question itself. Such sentences are called rhetorical sentences. They are often used in Public speeches to create effect on the audience.

e.g.: Who does not accept a bribe in modern days?
(Every one accepts)
Who has not heard about Mal atma Gandhi?
(Every one has heard)

A sentence is a combination of phrases and clauses.

A 'phrase' is a group of words without a finite verb but doing the work of a part of speech like a noun, adverb and adjective. Thus we have three kinds of phrases. 1. Noun phrase 2. Adverb Phrase and 3. Adjective Phrase.

1. Noun Phrases come as subjects in sentences.

e.g.: **To err** is human.
Walking a mile early in the morning is a good exercise.

In the above sentences 'to err', 'walking a mile earlier in the morning' are noun phrases coming as subjects of the sentences.

47

2. **Adverb Phrases** modify the verbs to which they refer.

    e.g.:   They went **round the garden**
              The river flows **through the heart** of the city.
              Students hurried **into the class room.**

3. **Adjective Phrases** qualify a noun or pronoun to which they refer.

    e.g.:   The captain **of the ship** was drowned.
              Napoleon became **Emperor** of France.
              A bride **in the hand** is worth two **in the bush.**

CLAUSES

Clauses are groups of words similar to phrases, acting like single parts of speech. But they have a subject and predicate of their own. A clause has a finite verb of its own whereas a phrase has no such verb. When a clause can stand on its own and independent it is called an INDEPENDENT CLAUSE OR MAIN CLAUSE.

SUBORDINATE CLAUSES are those clauses which cannot stand alone but depend for their meaning on the main clause.

e.g.:   I will come **when I am ready.**

Here 'when I am ready' modifies the verb 'will come' and indicates the time of coming. Therefore it is an ADVERB CLAUSE.

e.g.: I know that **I am not wrong.**

Here 'that I am not wrong' is the object of the verb 'know'. So it acts as a noun and hence is called a NOUN CLAUSE.

e.g.: Show me the figure **that you have painted**

Here 'that you have painted' qualifies the noun 'figure' before it and acts as an adjective. Hence it is called as an ADJECTIVE CLAUSE.

KINDS OF SUBORDINATE CLAUSES

There are three kinds of subordinate clauses. They are (1) Noun Clause (2) Adverb Clause and (3) Adjective Clause.

1. NOUN CLAUSE may be used as
    (a) subject (b) object
    (c) Predicatively (d) in opposition.

    a. **That he is honest** is well known.
        (subject)

    b. He told me **that he was ill.**
        (object)

    c. My opinion is **that he is right**
        (predicatively used or complement)

    d. I am unshakable in my belief **that he will come**
        (in opposition to belief)

2. ADVERB CLAUSES are of the following kinds:

    a. **Time Clause** introduced by conjunctions like 'after, as before, till, until, whenever, while, since. Phrases like as soon as, no sooner than etc.

        As I was returning home I slipped.
        After I left for Madras situation changed at home.

    b. **Place Clause** indicates location or space.

    e.g.: please stay **where you are**

    c. **Reason Clause** introduced by words like as, because, since, therefore, phrases like because of, on account of etc.

    e.g.: **Because he worked hard** he succeeded.
        Since it is sunday I enjoy holiday.

d. Purpose Clause is introduced by so..that, in order that, lest, in order to etc.

e.g.: We work hard **so that we may win the prize.**
He ran fast **lest** he might miss the bus.

e. Result or Consequence clause is introduced by 'so..that', 'such..that' 'too..to' in phrase.

e.g.: He ran **so** fast **that** he was out of breath.
His music was **so** wonderful **that** we were all entranced.

f. Condition Clause is introduced by words like 'if', in case, in case of, with, without and unless etc.

e.g.: **If you work hard** you will pass.
In case you hear me you will understand.
Unless you are ill you can easily digest this.

g. Concession Clause is introduced by 'though, although, even though, in spite of etc.

e.g.: Though he is poor he is honest.
Eventhough he is clever he is lazy.

h. Comparison Clause is introduced by 'as, than' etc.

e.g.: He behaved **as I expected**
He is not as bad **as I expected**
He is older **than I am**

3. ADJECTIVE CLAUSES are introduced by relative pronouns or relative adverbs often the relative pronoun is omitted in the accusative case.

e.g.: He **who works hard** will surely win.
He is the person **whom I want.**

EXERCISE

1. What is a sentence?

2. How many kinds of sentences are there? Give examples.

3. What is a phrase?

4. How many kinds of phrases are there?

5. Define a clause.

6. Differentiate between a main clause and subordinate clause.

7. How many kinds of subordinate clauses are there? What are they?

8. Give a list of the main subordinate clauses with examples.

9. What is a noun clause?

10. In what different ways can you use noun clause?

11. What is an adjective clause? Give examples.

12. Define an adverb clause.

13. What are the kinds of adverb clauses? Give examples to illustrate each type.

14. Point out the noun clauses in the following and explain how they are used.

51

    a. It appears that his directions were disobeyed.

    b. He could not understand why the experiment failed.

    c. History tells us how the town was attacked.

    d. The main question at issue is when he will clear the loan.

    e. The sense that he was alone grew upon him.

15. Point out the adverb clauses and the type to which they belong.

    a. As he was running to catch the bus he was arrested.

    b. When he met me I told him the whole story.

    c. He is so tall that he cannot walk straight.

    d. students attend college so that they may get their degree.

    e. If you are alert you can avoid the accident.

    f. Although he is dull he is brilliant at times.

16. Point out the adjective clauses in the following:

    a. The bag that is white is mine.

    b. He who starts early reaches early.

    c. The matter which is discussed is not very important.

    d. Gopi who is my friend is the monitor of the class.

    e. The hand that rocks the cradle rules the world.

CHAPTER XII
FORMS OF SENTENCES

THERE are three forms of sentences

1. **Simple Sentence**
2. **Complex Sentence**
3. **Compound Sentence**

1. **SIMPLE SENTENCE** consists of a single main clause or independent clause. It may or may not have phrases.

    e.g.: a. Rama killed Ravana.

    b. **In spite of his best efforts** he did not succeed.
       (phrase)

2. **COMPLEX SENTENCE** has only ONE MAIN CLAUSE and ONE or MORE SUBORDINATE CLAUSES. There may or may not be phrases. The subordinate clauses can be either Noun, Adjective or Adverb clauses according to need and situation.

    e.g.: a. He told me **that the college is closed**
                (Noun Clause)

    b. Students **who prepare well** write their examinations **with confidence**.

Here who prepare well is an adjective clause qualifying the noun 'students' 'with confidence' is a phrase.

    c. **After seeing the picture** he retired to bed.
       (Adverb Clause)

53

3. Compound sentence consists of two or more MAIN CLAUSES and one or more subordinate clauses.

A compound sentence having only two main clauses is called a DOUBLE SENTENCE.

e.g.: **He was clever** but very lazy.

Here two main clauses are joined by the conjunction 'but'.

Rama and Krishna joined the same college in the city **so that they may keep company in college also.**
Adv. Clause.

ANALYSIS OF SENTENCES

Analysis of sentences is the breaking up of every sentence into its constituent parts like the main clause and subordinate clause. After separating the subordinate clause, one has to point out what kind of subordinate clause it is. The function of the subordinate clause according to its being a noun, adjective or adverb clause should be clearly explained.

e.g.: a. That he is honest is well known.
    (it) is well known - Main Clause
    That he is honest - Noun Clause
    Subject of the verb **is well known.**

There is only one main clause and one subordinate clause. Therefore this is a COMPLEX SENTENCE.

b. With all my efforts I gained only a little.
    I gained only a little - Main clause.
    With all my efforts - Phrase.

There is only one main clause and a phrase. Therefore this is a simple sentence.

> c. We went to the picture and sat in the theatre for 2½ hours but were sadly disappointed.
> Here, we went to the picture - Main Clause
> We sat in the theatre for 2½ hrs. - Main Clause
> We were disappointed   - Main Clause
> And, But join the sentences.
> Therefore it is a Compound Multiple Sentence.

Opposite of ANALYSIS is SYNTHESIS or combination of sentences. The combination can be either in simple, complex or compound sentences.

By using phrases, clauses and other words the main clauses can be converted into sub clauses and phrases according to the requirement.

Simple to Complex

> a. There were certainly many dangers in coming to see the carnival. (Simple)
> There were certainly many dangers if you come to see the carnival (Sub. Clause) (Complex Sentence)

> b. Coming very late he lost his chance. (Simple)
> Because he came very late he lost his chance. (Complex)

> c. On reaching the destination he met his friend. (Simple)
> After he reached his destination he met his friend (Complex)

> d. He is too tall to walk straight (Simple)
> He is so tall that he cannot walk straight. (Complex)

55

   e. We attend college to take our degree. (Simple)
      We attend college so that we may take our degree.
      (Complex)

   f. Only with hard work you will succeed (Simple)
      Unless you work hard you will not succeed (Complex)

   g. In spite of his riches he is honest (Simple)
      Though he is rich he is honest. (Complex)

Compound to Simple

   a. He is not only an orator but also a philosopher.
      (Compound)
      He is both a philosopher and orator. (Simple)

   b. Either you do or die. (Compound)
      Before dying you do. (Simple)

   c. He is very clever but poor. (Compound)
      Inspite of his cleverness he is poor. (Simple)

   d. He came; he saw; he conquered. (Compound)
      Coming and seeing he conquered. (Simple)

Complex to Simple

   a. After he retired he bought the house. (Complex)
      After retirement he bought the house. (Simple)

   b. When he met his friend he was unconscious. (Complex)
      At the time of meeting his friend he unconscious.
      (Simple)

   c. Because he was ill he was hospitalized. (Complex)
      Because of his illness he was hospitalized. (Simple)

d. He was so good that he could not make profit. (Complex)
He was too good to make profit. (Simple)

e. In order that he may win I gave him my help. (Complex)
I gave him help to win. (Simple)

f. Though he is honest he is lazy. (Complex)
Inspite of his honesty he is lazy. (Simple)

Complex to Compound

a. After he met me he vanished. (Complex)
He met me and soon vanished (Compound)

b. Because you wanted I gave you the chance. (Simple)
You wanted and I gave you the chance. (Compound)

c. If you listen you will benefit (Complex)
Listen and you will benefit (Compound)

d. Although he is great he is mean sometimes. (Complex)
He is great but mean sometimes. (Compound)

e. He is a lover of music though he likes dance. (Complex)
He is not only a lover of music but likes dance also. (Compound)

EXERCISE

1. How many forms of sentences are there? What are they?

2. Define Simple, Complex and Compound Sentences. Give examples.

3. What is Analysis?

4. What is Synthesis?

5. Analyse the following sentences into main clauses and subordinate clauses and explain the construction of the subordinate clause.

   a. These transactions made him a rich man in a few years.

   b. There were several questions before the committee.

   c. A man, evidently in a state of intoxication, followed him to the door.

   d. The sea lay before us like a vast mirror.

   e. Our first care was to feed the animal.

   f. To his circle of readers his position now became one of extreme difficulty.

   g. Beyond that point there was for a time nothing but the roughest of foot paths.

h. To the last carrying for the house was done by the two big New Zealand Pack Horses.

i. A small bed stead, a couple of book cases, a plain deal kitchen table and two chairs were all its furniture.

j. In a corner I caught a glimpse of my guide.

Analyse the following sentences and say what forms of sentences they are:

a. He said that the right of self determination is the most important thing.

b. He sent out to the factories of the company orders that no indulgence should be shown to the intruders.

c. It appears that his directions were obeyed.

d. That he will surely win the match was already known to many.

e. He could not understand why the experiment was a failure.

f. As soon as the teacher entered the class all the boys stood up.

g. He got the first rank because he worked very hard before the examinations.

h. He reached the station well in advance so that he may catch the train.

i. They are so alert that none can escape.

j. If you are worthy you will surely find a place in the list.

k. Though he is poor he is honest.

l. Either you act now or miss it totally.

m. He is not only a villain but also a rogue.

n. Neither my father nor my brother wanted to see me.

Combine the following into one sentence (either simple or complex)

a. He told me. The shop is closed today.

b. Rama came. Rama spoke of his problem. Krishna promised to help him.

c. The bag is white in colour. It is mine.

d. The master is clever. He lives in my house in a portion.

e. His name cannot be forgotten. Gandhi sacrificed himself for Hindu Muslim Unity.

CHAPTER XIII
ARTICLES

$\mathbf{A}$, **An** and **The** are called ARTICLES. In fact they are demonstrative adjectives.

A, An are called INDEFINITE articles because they do not speak of anything definite.

> *e.g.:* a doctor, a boy, a chair, a table etc.

'The' is called DEFINITE article as it refers to some thing definite or specific or particular.

> *e.g.:* the boy, the doctor, the chair etc.
> (Particular boy, doctor, chair etc.)

The use of A or An depends upon the sound. An is used before a vowel sound.

> *e.g.:* an enemy
> an ink stand
> an ass
> an umbrella
> an hour

A is used before a consonantal sound.

> *e.g.:* a boy, a university, a yard, a hole, a European etc.

In words with 'h' at the beginning, if 'h' is silent 'an' can be used.

> *e.g.:* an historical novel, an hotel.

USAGE OF DEFINITE ARTICLE

a. The Definite Article is used to show a particular person or thing.

e.g.: I dislike **the** fellow.

b. To show a singular noun representing a whole class.

e.g.: **The** cow is a useful animal.

c. With names of gulfs, rivers, seas, oceans, groups of islands and mountain ranges.

e.g.: **the** Persian Gulf, **the** Ganges, **the** Red Sea, **the** Indian Ocean, **the** Himalayas, **the** Andamans etc.

d. Before common nouns of unique nature.

e.g.: **the** sun, **the** moon, **the** sky, **the** ocean, **the** earth.

e. Before superlatives and ordinals.

e.g.: **The darkest** cloud has a silverlining.
The third chapter of the novel is good.

f. Before adjectives when the noun is understood.

e.g.: **The** poor are always forgotten.

g. As an adverb with comparatives.

e.g.: **The** more the **merrier** .

INDEFINITE ARTICLE is used

1. In the sense of one

e.g.: Not **a** word was said.

2. In a vague uncertainity

e.g.: **A** beggar came. (somebody)

3. In the sense of any

   e.g.: **A** cow is a useful animal.

4. to make a common noun of a proper noun.

   e.g.: He is **a** Daniel come to judgement.
   He is **a** Napoleon in fight.
   He is **a** Gandhi in determination.

OMISSION OF INDEFINITE ARTICLE

a. Before a common noun used in its widest meaning.

   e.g.: Man is mortal

b. Before names of material and proper nouns.

   e.g.: Gold is a precious metal.
   Bombay is a big city.

c. Before abstract nouns used in a general sense.

   e.g.: Honesty is the best policy.
   Knowledge is power.

EXERCISE

Fill up the blanks with suitable 'articles'.

1. He is ..... great man.

2. ..... box was selected by me.

3. ..... elephant is considered ..... holy beast.

4. ..... sun rises in ..... east.

5. She is ..... first girl in the class.

6. ...... Taj is ..... most beautiful building in ..... world.

7. He is ..... Daniel come to judgement.

8. Honesty is ..... best policy.

9. ..... Himalayas are ..... highest mountains in ...... world.

10. ..... Andamans are ..... group of islands in ..... Bay of Bengal.

CHAPTER XIV
AUXILIARY VERBS

THESE are also called helping verbs and are used generally in the formation of future tense (especially shall and will).

I.   The verb 'am, was, been' is used

    a. as a verb with full meaning

    e.g.: I am a research scholar.

    b. as an auxiliary

    i. 'am' etc with the present participle, forms continuous tenses.

    e.g.: I am writing
           I am walking
           I am seeing   etc.

    ii. 'am' with past participle forms the passive voice.

    e.g.: I am seen, etc.

II. The verb 'do, did, done' is used -

    a. as a verb of full meaning

    e.g.: He did his job

    b. With the infinitive in the present tense as an auxiliary in compound forms of the present and past active.

    e.g.: I did enjoy it (emphatic)
           Do you like it? (Interrogative)
           You did not listen (Negative)

III. The verb 'have, had' is used -

    a. as a verb of complete meaning

    e.g.:   He has a lot of property

    b. With the past participle as an auxiliary to form perfect tenses

    e.g.:   I have seen the picture.
             I shall have walked etc.

IV. The verb 'may, might' is used -

    a. as a verb of full meaning, with infinitive as object -

    e.g.:   You may (are allowed to) go.
             He may do the job   etc.

    b. as an auxiliary, with an infinitive (without to) as a subjunctive equivalent.

    e.g.:   He went to Simla in order that he might recoup his health.

V. The Verbs shall and will

    a. shall and will are used as auxiliaries to express mere futurity. They are used with infinitives to form future tenses.

    e.g.:   I shall go; you will go; He will go, We shall go; They will go;

The past tenses 'should and would' are similarly used to form future in the past tenses.

    b. 'will' in the First Person, and 'shall' in the Second and Third are used as verbs of full meaning followed by an infinitive to express determination, obligation, a promise or a threat.

e.g.: I will go (i.e. am determined to go) whether you like it or not.
He shall go to the doctor (I have decided that he shall go)

c. Care must be taken not to confuse the tense of these verbs in the same sentence.

If 'shall or will' is used in the main clause, 'shall or will' must be used in the subordinate 'if' clause. If 'should or would' is used in the main clause 'should or would' must be used in the subordinate clause. (If)

e.g.: I shall be grateful to you if you will send me the goods early.

VI. DEFECTIVE VERBS are those verbs which do not have certain forms and therefore cannot be completely conjugated.

Examples of Defective Verbs

shall	can	need
will	dare	ought
may	must	

I can **do** this.
Dare you **see** my friend?
She need not **worry** about that.
They ought **to understand** perfectly.

In these sentences the verbs do, see, worry, to know are all Infinitives used as objects of the defective verbs.

EXERCISE

1. Give the various uses of the verbs am, do, have, may, shall, will

   a. as verbs of full meaning

   b. as auxiliaries.

2. a. What are defective verbs?

   b. Why are they so called?

   c. What part of the verb is 'do' in the sentence, "I can do this"?

CHAPTER XV
DIRECT AND INDIRECT (REPORTED) SPEECH

DIRECT Speech indicates the exact words of the speaker in the FIRST PERSON and marked off by inverted commas.

Indirect Speech is the speech of the person as quoted or reported by someone else. It is therefore introduced by a verb of saying or reporting verb like 'He said that, etc. Indirect speech is always in THIRD PERSON.

> e.g.: The teacher said, I am very busy now (Direct)
> The teacher said that he was very busy then.
> (Indirect)

Here we find a few changes in the Indirect Speech.

1. The Conjunction 'that' is used before the indirect statement.

2. The pronoun 'I' is changed to 'he' (first person to third person)

3. The verb 'am' is changed to 'was' (present tense changed to past tense)

4. The adverb 'now is changed to 'then'.

Rules for changing Direct into Indirect or Reported Speech

a. Pronouns as a rule must be in the third person for Reported Speech.

b. When the Reporting Verb is in the past tense every present tense in the direct speech must be changed into its corresponding past form.

   e.g.:   i.   Rama said, I am unwell (Direct)
                   Rama said that he was unwell (Indirect)

         ii.   The servant said, **My** master is **writing** letters (Direct)
               The servant said that **his** master **was writing** letters. (Indirect)

        iii. Krishana said, **I have passed**the examination . (Direct)
               Krishna said that **he had passed** examination. (Indirect)

Shall and **will** of the future tense are changed to **should** and **would**.

c. If the main or reporting verb is in the present tense, the tenses in the Direct Speech do not change.

The above examples can be written as

   i.   Rama says that he is unwell. (Indirect)

   ii.   The servant says that his master is writing letters. (Indirect)

   iii. Krishna says that he has passed the examination. (Indirect)

d. All pronouns, adjectives or adverbs showing nearness must be replaced by the words denoting corresponding remoteness.

   e.g.:   This is what these statesmen are doing now (Direct Speech)

(He said that) that was what those statesmen were doing then (Indirect)

Direct		Indirect
now	becomes	then
here	"	there
ago	"	before
thus	"	so
today	"	that day
tomorrow	"	the next day
yesterday	"	the day before
last night	"	the night before
this	"	that
these	"	those

e. Direct questions are changed into Indirect questions with the help of verbs like 'asked, inquired, enquired' etc

> *e.g.:* He said to me, What are you doing ? (Direct)
> He asked me what I was doing (Indirect)
>
> Where do you live? asked the man (Direct)
> The man enquired where I lived. (Indirect)
>
> Jane said, Will you listen to such a man?
> (Direct)
> Jane asked them whether they would listen to such a man (Indirect)

f. Direct commands become dependent commands requiring an introduction or they may be reported by using let' with the infinitive.

e.g.: The teacher said, "Rama, Go away" (Direct).
The teacher ordered Rama to go away. (Indirect)

Somu told his friend, "Please wait here till I
return"   (Direct)

Somu requested his friend to wait there till he
returned   (Indirect)

g. While reporting exclamations and wishes suitable
verbs expressing the same ideas are used.

e.g.: He said, "Alas! I am undone"   (Direct)
He exclaimed sadly that he was undone
                                         (Indirect)

Susan said, "How clever I am"   (Direct)
Susan exclaimed that she was very clever.
                                         (Indirect)

EXERCISE

Change the following sentences into Indirect Speech

1. He says, "I do not simply say that I tolerate
   religions. That is an insult to god. I accept all
   religions".

2. "All paths lead to me", it says.

3. "Of making books there is no end", complained
   the preacher.

4. As we drove off I said, "What dirty swine!"

5. "Chase them", he shouted.

6. "Don't be mad", my brother said.

7. My father said, "you people make me sick!"

8. He said, "Gently brother, I was once a hotel owner myself".

9. "Glad to meet you", I said then trying to hide my nervousness, I added, "How are you?"

10. "Ah, it is as we suspected preplanned and organized to crush us" another section cried.

11. The health officer no doubt came and said, "you must put all this under glass lid, otherwise I shall destroy it all some day ...... take care!"

12. He said, "It was only a bit of function you had no right to swear at us".

13. "No, Sabib, No", he said ' you must not burn these papers for I am now your slave.

14. My father said, "How dare you shout at me like that?"

CHAPTER XVI
USAGE OF SIMPLE PREPOSITIONS

1. IN is used for large countries and towns.

2. AT is used for small towns and villages.

   e.g.: He lives **in** Delhi.
   I live **in** Madras **at** Perambur

3. IN, AT speak of things at rest.

4. TO, INTO speak of things in motion.

   e.g.: Ramu is **in** bed.
   John is **at** the top of the class.
   He jumped **into** the well.
   I ran **to** him.

5. ON speaks of rest.

6. UPON speaks of motion.

   e.g.: They sat **on** the cot.
   The dog sprang **upon** the table.

7. TILL speaks of time

8. TO speaks of place

e.g.: Shyam slept **till** 8 o'Clock.
They came **to** the end of the street.

9. WITH speaks of instrument.
BY speaks of agent.

e.g.: He killed two birds **with** one shot.
He was stabbed **by** a stranger.

EXERCISE

Fill up the blanks with suitable prepositions

1. I intend ..... come and stay ..... you a week.

2. The book is ..... the table.

3. He went out ..... a walk.

4. He is fond ..... tea

5. The engine gives ...... smoke.

6. He is one ...... the many citizens.

7. The bridge is ..... the river

8. The church is ...... our house.

9. I do not know much .... him

10. ...... the tree there is a large area of shelter.

CHAPTER XVII
PUNCTUATION

T HE word punctuation comes from the latin word 'punctee' which means a point. Therefore punctuation is the right or proper use of putting in points or stops in writing.

The main marks of punctuation are

1. Full stop or period (.)
2. Comma (,)
3. Semicolon (;)
4. Colon (:)
5. Interrogative mark (?)
6. Exclamatory mark (!)
7. Inverted commas or ("") quotation marks
8. The dash (−)
9. Apostrophe (')

1. a. The **full stop** is used for a complete pause and separation.

   b. It is used at the end of a declarative or an imperative sentence (order, request).

   c. It is used to mark abbreviations and initials.
   e.g.: M.A., M.P.

In current English Mr. Mrs. are written without a full stop.

   e.g.: Mr, Mrs

2. **a.** The **comma** is the shortest pause. It is used to separate a series of words in the sentence construction.

   e.g.: They lost lands, money, reputation and friends.

   b. It is used to separate each pair of words connected by 'and'.

   e.g.: We should be devout and humble, cheerful and serene.

3. The **semicolon** is used for a stop more important than that indicated by the comma.

   e.g.: He was a brave, large hearted man; and we all liked him.
   His heart was pure; his life serene

4. **Colon** represents a more important stop than the semicolon. It is introduced before a quotation.

   e.g.: Bacon says: Reading makes a full man, writing an exact man, speaking a ready man .

5. The mark of **Interrogation** is used at the end of a direct question.

   e.g.: What is your name?
   Have you done your work?

6. The **Exclamatory** mark is used after interjections and words and phrases expressing sudden emotions.

   e.g.: Alas! Oh! Hurrah! Ah! etc.

7. **Inverted commas** are used to denote the exact words of a speaker (Direct speech) or quotation.

   e.g.: "I would rather die than beg at the other man's door"

8. The **Dash** is used to show an abrupt stop or change of thought and come back to a scattered subject.

    e.g.:   if Gandhi were alive - but why think of the past. Friends, followers, Kith and Kin - all left him.

9. The **Apostrophe** is used to show the omission of a letter or letters and the genetive or possessive case of nouns.

    e.g.: Don't, I've, He's ·

Capital letters are used

1. to start a sentence.

2. to start each fresh line in poetry.

3. for all proper nouns and adjectives derived from them.

    e.g.:   Madras, Rama, Asia, Shakespeare, Shakesperean

4. For all nouns and pronouns used to denote God.

    eg.:   The Lord, He is theGod Almighty

EXERCISE

Punctuate the following sentences

1. glad to meet you i said then trying to hide my feelings i added how are you.

2. believe me I know it I told him and it felt good to say that to some one.

3. he said it was thundering for a long time it has rained now.

4. we stopped my father said how dare you shout at me like that

5. michael what are you going to do my mother asked.

6. no Sahib no he said

7. i am fine the question is how are you

8. look he said why don't you draw a line a few inches behind the board and aim at making you take off from there.

CHAPTER XVIII
TAG QUESTIONS

$\mathbf{A}$ question tagged at the end of a sentence is called a tag question. This type of question is very common in conversation and serves the purpose of confirmation.

The two patterns of Tag Questions are:

1. Auxiliary Verb + not + subject if the sentence is in the positive or affirmative.

2. Auxiliary + subject if the statement is negative.

    e.g.: Venu broke the glass **did n't he?**
          Your aunt cooks well, **does n't she?**
          Mohan does n't work hard, **does he?**
          They have n't come yet, **have they?**

EXERCISE

Add question tags to the following:

1. He has his eyes in all his company.

2. He is patient

3. We live in a curious age.

4. Students are not supposed to be ignorant and stupid.

5. Women are special custodians of all that is pure and religious in life.

6. The message of the Gita is not sectarian.

7. They are testing man's faith.

8. And wars are not made by traditional groups.

9. He remembers the addresses of his friends.

10. We thought it was an accident.

CHAPTER XIX

TRANSFORMATION OF SENTENCES

(NEGATIVE & INTERROGATIVE OR RHETORICAL)

THE Assertive sentence or statement can be changed into a Negative Sentence. It is important to note that when such a change is made the meaning of the sentence remains unchanged.

e.g.:
  a. Rama loved Krishna. (Statement)
     Rama was not without love for Krishna (or)
     Rama did not hate Krishna (Negative)

  b. He is greater than I (Statement)
     I am not so great as he (Negative)

  c. He is an honest man (statement)
     He is not a dishonest man (Negative)

  d. Only a few attended the meeting (Statement)
     Not many attended the meeting (Negative)

  e. I have only a little money (Statement)
     I have not much money (Negative)

  f. He has little sense (Statement)
     He has no sense. (Negative)

  g. As soon as the head master came all the
     boys stood up (Statement)
     No sooner did the headmaster come than
     all the boys stood up. (Negative)

Two Negatives make an affirmative and give us the positive meaning.

> *e.g.:* It is **not** for **nothing** that he joined politics
> (It is only for something that he joined politics).

A. A Statement can be changed into a question by changing the word order. Usually such sentences are called Rhetorical Sentences. They do not expect any answer. The answer is implied and it is within the sentence.

> *e.g.:* a. No one can be expected to submit forever to injustice (Negative statement)
> Can any one be expected to submit forever to injustice? (No one can)
>
> b. Is there anything better than a busy life? (Rhetorical)
> There is nothing better than a busy life. (Statement)

EXERCISE

Change into Negative Sentences:

1. He is a friend of religious toleration.

2. He is too lazy to bear hatred.

3. You must, in a word, love these people.

4. She must refuse to adorn herself for men.

5. He is seldom prominent in conversation.

Change into Questions

1. There is really no substitute

2. His customers liked him.

3. It has done this in atleast two ways.

4. He never spoke to me on the subject.

5. The passing shows do not affect the reality.

CHAPTER XX
SYNONYMS AND ANTONYMS

S YNONYMS are words that have almost the same meaning -

e.g.:   battle, conflict, contest
colour, dye, paint
stain, tinge
acute, keen, sharp etc.

Synonyms appear to have the same meaning but there is subtle difference between words and their usages. For example the two words 'begin' and 'commence' convey different meanings. The word 'begin' is a simple. word and has a much wider usage where as the word 'commence' belongs to more pretentions language. In the same manner the two words 'rich' and 'wealthy' refers to persons having a great deal of money or property. 'Rich' is used in various ways as in 'rich jewellery, rich decorations, rich soil, rich in suggestions, etc.

ANTONYMS are words with opposite meanings.

e.g.:   young   x   old
rich   x   poor
friend   x   enemy
fast   x   slow
bright   x   dull
negligent x   careful
extricate x   involve
deprive   x   endow
sever   x   connect
consider   x   ignore

fluent	x	laboured
drive	x	coax
special	x	ordinary
mundane	x	spiritual
beautiful	x	ugly

A number of synonyms are used wrongly and carelessly. In some case the synonyms has both a primary and secondary meaning. Here is a list of synonyms which may be of use to students in general.

Aberration, deviation, wandering,

Absolute, not relative, unconditioned, unalterable

Accessory, additional, auxiliary, aiding

Achieve, accomplish, perform, gain

Acme, summit, highest point

Adept (at), proficient, skilled

Adherent, follower, partisan

Adhesive, sticky

Adventitious, accidental, casual

Aggravate, worsen

Alleviate, make light, mitigate, relieve

Ameliorate, make better, improve

Antithesis, contrast

Apathy, want of feeling, indifference

Appalling, terrifying, dreadful

Apposite, adapted, suitable

Appraise, value, estimate

Apprehend, seize, know, fear

Arbitrary, lawless, despotic, absolute

Cajole, persuade, flatter, deceit

Candid, sincere, ingenuous, honourable,

Casual, chance, uncertain

Catastrophe, disaster, calamity

Cogent, powerful, convincing

Colossal, gigantic, huge

Criterion, standard, test, rule

Crucial, testing, decisive

Cursory, hasty, superficial, careless

Desultory, discontinuous, irregular, rambling

Diffident, modest, bashful

Economy, management of money, frugality

Egotism, selfishness

Emulate, imitate, rival

Ephemeral, transient, short lived

Eradicate, destroy

Extravagant, unrestrained, excessive, wasteful

Fascinate, charm, enchant

Illicit, unlawful

Immaculate, spotless, innocent, guileless

Indigent, poor

Inexorable, resolved, relentless, inflexible

Innocuous, harmless

Insiduous, treacherous, false, cunning

Laconic, concise, pithy

Ludicrous, laughable, ridiculous

Morbid, diseased, unhealthy

Moribund, dying

Obliterate, efface, destroy

Penury, want, poverty

Permeate, passthrough, pervade

Plagiarism, theft

Plebeian, popular

Precocious, premature, forward

Reimburse, repay, refund

Reiterate, repeat

Reticent, silent, reserved

Satiate, satisfy, glut, cloy

Sedative, calming, soothing

Solicitude, anxiety, care

Spurious, false, illegitimate

Subsidiary, auxiliary, aiding

Sycophant, flatterer

Taciturn, silent, morose

Tentative, experimental, essaying

Tortuous, twisted, winding, deceitful

Unique, standing alone, single, unequalled

Urbane, polite, courteous, refined

Vacillate, waver, hesitate

Voracious, greedy

WORDS OF SIMILAR FORM BUT DIFFERENT MEANING

Many pairs of words are similar in form but different in meaning. Some of the commonest pairs are used in the sentences below:

1. **Adverse : Averse**

   e.g.:   Even in **adverse** conditions he was able to win. In spite of his want of knowledge he is not **averse** to reason.

2. **Affect : effect**

   e.g.:   These conditions will **affect** the result. He was hurt but **affected** indifference. What is the **effect** of this information?

3. **Alternate : Alternative**

   e.g.:   The worker is expected on **alternate** days (every otherday)

   There is no other **alternative** to hard work. (Substitute)

4. **Apposite : Opposite**

e.g.: His words were not **apposite** as we were discussing some other matter.
My friend has **opposite** views.

5. **Canvas : Canvass**

e.g.: The tent is made of **canvas** (water proof material)
He has to **canvass** for votes (plead)

6. **Compliment : Complement**

e.g.: We gave him our gift with best **compliments**
Nouns and adjectives are used as **complements** in a sentence.
(that which completes the meaning)

7. **Deficient : Defective**

e.g.: He is **deficient** in artistic talent.
The shoes are **defective**

8. **Deprecate : Depreciate**

e.g.: We **deprecate** indiscipline.
The value of machinery generally **depreciates** every year.

9. **Dominant : Dominate**

e.g.: His courage was **dominant** among those men.
The Chairman's speech **dominated** the proceedings.

10. **Expedient : Expeditious**

e.g.: Though the work was not to his liking he found it **expedient** to approve it.
Very important letters have to reach the governor **expediously**.

11. **Illegible : Ineligible**

   e.g.: Your handwriting is **illegible** (difficult to read)
   By failing in his examinations he has become **ineligible** for the scholarship and other concessions.

12. **Imperial : Imperious**

   e.g.: **Imperial** talks are held between King and their advisers.
   His manner is highly **imperious**.

13. **Judicious : Judicial**

   e.g.: His choice of books is always **judicious.**
   judicial affairs are looked after by my lawyer.

14. **Luxurious : Luxuriant**

   e.g.: He lives a **luxurious** life.
   She has a **luxuriant** growth of hair.

15. **Negligent : Negligible**

   e.g. : He is **negligent** in his studies.
   His mistakes are **negligible**.

16. **Notable : Notorious**

   e.g.: Indian scientists have **notable** contributions to their credit.
   Veerappan is a **notorious** bandit and sandal-wood smuggler.

17. **Official : Officious**

   e.g.: **Official** confirmation of his appointment has been received.
   He repeatedly offered his services where they were not wanted, until at last his chief told him not to be **officious**.

18. Practise : Practice

e.g.: He **practised** very well till he became an expert in the game.
Practice makes a man perfect.

19. Precipitate : Precipitous

e.g.: Do not **precipitate** matters by your argument.
The mountain track is highly **precipitous**

20. Principal : Principle

e.g.: The **Principal** of the college is a great scholar.
You have to repay according to the **principles** laid down.

21. Transitive : Transitory

e.g.: A **transitive** verb denotes an action exerted on an object.
Our earthly life is **transitory**.

22. Vocation : Avocation

e.g.: He has chosen teaching for his **vocation**
Gardening in his spare time is his **avocation**.

EXERCISE

1. What are synonyms and antonyms?
Give two examples for each.

2. Give the synonyms for the following words
   a. adept
   b. candid

    c. eradicate

    d. illicit

    e. moribund

    f. penury

    g. vacillate

3. Give the antonyms of the following
    a. negligent

    b. extricate

    c. deprive

    d. sever

    e. fluent

    f. mundane

    g. drive

4. Use the following pairs in sentences so as to bring out their meanings.
    a. Canvas : Canvass

    b. Apposite : Opposite

    c. Compliment : Complement

    d. Illegible : Ineligible

CHAPTER XXI
IDIOMS AND PHRASES

IDIOMS are Phrases which have a special meaning as a whole though they are formed from different parts of speech. They may be noun, adjectival or adverbial phrases. They can also be prepositional phrases formed by the combination of verbs and prepositions. Generally verbs combine with different prepositions and give different meanings. The verb is the same but the prepositions change and change the entire meaning of the phrase or idiom.

e.g.:

$$\text{Give} \longrightarrow \begin{cases} \text{up} \\ \text{way} \\ \text{away} \quad \text{etc.} \\ \text{in} \end{cases}$$

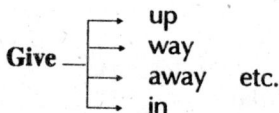

Mistakes in using prepositional phrases are very common. The right preposition should be used to bring in the full force of the idiom. Any other preposition used after the verb is a mistake and does not bring in the correct meaning or idea. Therefore it is better to study the correct usage of prepositions in idioms and phrases.

The following sentences indicate the correct usage of prepositions after certain words.

1. His conduct does not **admit of** excuse.
2. He does not **agree with** his opinion.
3. They do not **agree to** his suggestion.
4. I **acquiesce in** his decision.

5. He is not **amenable to** reason.

6. He is **averse to** doing the job.

7. Your conduct is not **compatible with** Indian culture.

8. They together **Connived at** the theft.

9. She is **deficient in** social qualities.

10. He is **different from** others.

11. I have a **distaste for** modern politics.

12. Canvas is **impervious to** water.

13. He has no **influence over** the chief minister.

14. My brother is **impatient with** others who object his ideas.

15. He is **inspired by** love for others.

16. We must **instill into** children the quality of patriotism.

17. Don't **intrude on** others rights.

18. He is **independent of** his father.

19. He acted **irrespective of** my wishes.

20. He is **ineligible for** promotion.

21. He continued **oblivious of** any count of time.

22. Coffee is **preferable to** Tea

23. I could not attend the function as I was **preoccupied with** urgent business.

24. I **prevail upon** you to stay here for a couple of days more.

25. The bitter enemies finally **reconciled with** each other. One has to **reconcile** himself **to** his fate.

26. You are **responsible for** your son's future. The ministers are **responsible to** the parliament.

27. People are not **satisfied with** politicians.

28. His remarks **savour** of hypocrisy.

29. He was **profuse in** his comments.

30. His radical opinion will **militate against** his progress.

CERTAIN WORDS FREQUENTLY MISUSED

1. Aggravate should be used to mean 'to increase the gravity of' 'to make worse'.

    e.g.: His illness was **aggravated** by the wet climate.

    The word 'Individual' should not be used as a synonym for 'person'. An individual is a single, separate person as opposed to group.

    e.g.: In dictatorship absolute power is in the hands of an **individual**.

2. **Mutual** is often misused for 'common'. The word implies an action or relation between two or more persons or things.

    e.g.: The two men could never work together because of **mutual** suspicion.

3. **Nice** is used as a substitute for many different adjectives. A nice day, a nice hat, a nice mess, a nice man, a nice taste etc. The meaning has become vague. It is better to use the precise adjective required by the context.

4. **Transpire** is wrongly used as a synonym for 'happen'. The exact meaning is 'breathe through', 'become known'.

    e.g.: What **'transpired'** between the two friends and their talk are not known.

5. **Unique** implies that there is nothing precisely similar to it in existence. When used it must not be qualified by an adverb.

   Other adjectives that do not admit of comparison are : 'square', 'golden', 'round', 'universal' and 'preferable'.

6. **'Idea'** should never be used to mean plan or principle, cause or scheme.

7. **'Differ'** must not be confused with 'vary'. The correct usuage is 'differ from' not 'differ according to'. 'vary' can be used with 'according to'.

8. **Indulge in** should apply only to pleasures or amusements. It should not be used to mean 'engaged in'.

9. **Asset** is a pure technical term. It should not be used to mean any possession or advantage.

10. **The latter** always refers to the second of two things or persons. It is always better to use the word in conjunction with 'the former'

11. **Populace** must not be confused with 'People' or 'Population'. The word means 'the common people, the rabble'.

12. **Percentage** is wrongly used for 'Number' 'Proportion'. The word is purely mathematical.

13. **Protagonist** means a chief actor in a drama or story (Greek : Protos, first; Agonistic, actor; Therefore it has come to mean a leading person in a struggle for some cause).

    e.g.: She was the protagonist in the campaign for women's political rights.

14. **Disinterested** is often confused with 'un interested'. Actually 'disinterested' has the meaning of detached or impartial.

15. **Exotic** does not mean 'luxurious' or 'lavish'. Properly it means 'introduced from abroad'. It is applied to fashions, plants and words.

EXERCISE

1. What are idioms and phrases?

2. Illustrate the correct use of prepositions with phrases from any five of the prepositional phrases.

3. Give five examples of important words often confused and misused. Give their correct usage.

PART 2

COMPOSITION

CHAPTER XXII
PARAPHRASING

PARAPHRASING can be considered as a translation of a particular passage into another form of words in simple and clearer language. A paraphrase should not be confused with a precis. Precis involves condensation but a paraphrase is faithful to the original sentence by sentence without omitting any of the thought.

A good practice in paraphrasing will be to reproduce in one's own words the sense of a short passage as given below:

1. A stitch in time saves nine (Proverb)

Paraphrase:

A little trouble taken early will save a great deal of trouble later on.

2. A pithy saying or quotation or witty remark.

Some books are to be tasted, others to be swallowed and some few to be chewed and digested (Bacon).

Paraphrase

Some books deserve to be lightly read; others may be read through rapidly at a sitting; a few require close study for the proper understanding and assimilation of the author's ideas.

Paraphrasing Poetry

Frequently paraphrasing passages are in verse. We find in poetry a changed word order, vocabulary, figures of speech, etc. that are not used generally in prose. Therefore paraphrases of a poetic passage must be examples of simplicity and normality of expression. The following passages illustrate the method of paraphrasing poetry.

PASSAGE

Example 1

> In full blown dignity see Wolsey stand,
> Law in his voice and fortune in his hand.
> To him the church, the realm, their pavers consign.
> Through him the rays of regal bounty shine;
> Turned by his nod the stream of honour flows.
> His smile alone security bestows;
> Still to new heights his restless wishes tower;
> Claim leads to claim and Power advances Power;
> Till conquest unresisted ceased to please,
> And rights submitted left have none to seize.
>
> *(Dr. Johnson)*

Paraphrase:

See Wolsey at the height of his glory; his word is law and his hand bestows honours. Both Church and the State have handed over their powers to him and he is the means by which the King's favours are conferred. His nod is enough to give preference to a man and his smile alone will make a man safe in his position. He is ever restless and aspiring to new heights. Each claim leads to another and every fresh acquisition of power gives the means for further attempts, until at last conquest becomes so easy that it brings no pleasure and so many rights are given up to him that there are none left to seize.

PASSAGE

Example 2:

Westminister Bridge 1802

Earth has not anything to show more fair:
Dull would be he of soul who could pass by
A sight so touching in its majesty:
This city now doth, like a garment, wear.
The beauty of the morning; silent, bare,
Ships, towers, domes, theatres and temples lie
Open into the fields and to the sky.
All bright and glittering in the smokeless air.
Never did Sun more beautifully steep.
In his first splendour, valley, rock or hill;
Ne'er saw I, never felt, a calm so deep!
The river glideth at his own sweet will:
Dear God! the very houses seem asleep;
And all that mighty heart is lying still!

(Wordsworth)

Paraphrase

Nothing on earth is fairer than this and he who could pass on unmoved by such a majestic sight must lack all the finer qualities. London appears most beautiful in the bright morning light. Ships and buildings of all kinds stretching out towards the fields, stand silent against the sky and all shine brightly in the smokeless air. Not even wild hill and valley bathed in early morning sunlight present a more splendid picture than this. Never have I seen or felt so deep a calm. The river flows peacefully on, undisturbed by any craft. Even the houses seem asleep and all that great human society is at rest.

THE METHOD OF PARAPHRASING

1. Read the passage twice or thrice to get a clear idea of the general meaning.

2. Make notes of words or phrases which are poetical and need to be changed.

3. Follow the original, sentence by sentence and make a rough draft of your paraphrase.

4. Compare the draft with the original. Find out if you have faithfully rendered the meaning of the poetical passage into prose. Make any changes if necessary.

5. Read the paraphrase, without reference to the original and find out if it is written in simple, good, idiomatic English that can be read easily and understood.

HOW TO PARAPHRASE POETRY

1. For all words and phrases that are uncommon or archaic. Substitute words or phrases in common use.

2. Where it is essential rearrange the parts of sentences so as to get the normal prose order.

3. Long sentences must be broken up into shorter ones. The punctuation of the paraphrase will be different from the original.

4. Remove highly figurative expressions and replace them by simple common expressions.

5. According to necessity a sentence or two can be expanded. As poetry is terse the idea of the poet cannot be properly expressed without expansion in more words.

6. Don't try to use a synonym for every word in the original. Sometimes the original word is the best and the only one possible.

7. Do not alter the person of the original.

HOW TO PARAPHRASE PROSE

Though the method is the same as for paraphrasing poetry other difficulties may arise.

a. The language may require to be simplified.

b. The passage may be in archaic style and so should be rewritten in modern English.

c. The passage may contain long, involved sentences, which for clarity, should be subdivided.

d. The thought of the passage may be difficult. The paraphrase writer should show that he has grasped the meaning and can express it in his own words.

103

Example

Paraphrase into Modern English

Monday, the Ninth of September, in the after noon, the frigate was near cast away oppressed by waves, but at the time recovered, and giving forth signs of joy, the general, sitting about with a book in his hand, cried unto us in the 'Hinde' so often as we did approach within hearing, 'we are as near to heaven by sea as by land' 'reiterating the same speech, well be seeming a soldier resolute in Jesus Christ, as I can testify that he was. The same Monday night, about twelve of the clock or not long after, the frigate being ahead of us in the 'Golden Hinde' suddenly her lights were out, where of as it were in a moment we lost the sight; and with all our watch cried. "The General was cast away; which was too true".

(Hakluyt)

PARAPHRASE

On the afternoon of Monday, the ninth of September, the frigate was in such difficulties owing to the high seas that she nearly foundered. Throughout that afternoon, however, she managed to keep afloat. The General, who was sitting abaft with a book in his hand, made signs of joy at her escape and as often as we in the "Hinde" approached within hearing distance, he shouted to us, "we are as near to heaven by seas as by land. These words of encouragement, which he uttered again and again, were most fitting in the mouth of a soldier who was so faithful a Christian, as I can testify he was. The same Monday night about 12 o'clock or shortly after, the frigate was sailing ahead of us in the "Golden Hind", when suddenly her lights went out and were seen no more. At this our watch cried out, The General is cast away ! - and it was all too true.

EXERCISE

Give the meaning of the following in your own words.

a. A rolling stone gathers no moss.

b. Still waters run deep.

c. Make hay while the sun shines.

d. A bird in the hand is worth two in the bush.

e. Where ignorance is bliss
'Tis folly to be wise.

f. The mind is its own place, and in itself.
Can make a Heaven of Hell, a Hell of Heaven.

g. There is a divinity doth shape our ends
Rough-hew them how we will.

h. One crowded hour of glorious life.
Is worth an age without a name.

i. Of great riches there is no real use except it be in the distribution.

j. A man young in years may be old in hours, if he have lost no time.

Paraphrase the following:

a. For him light labour spread her wholesome store. Just gave what life required, but gave no more: His best companions Innocence and Health; And his best riches ignorance of wealth. But times are altered; trades unfeeling train Usurp the land and disposses the swain. Along the lawn, where scattered hamlets rose, Unwidely wealth and cumbrous Pomp repose. Those healthy sports that graced the peaceful scene, Lived in each look and brightened all the green; These far departing seek a kinder shore, And rural mirth and manners are no more.

(Goldsmith)

b. Not always Actions show the man: we find who does a Kindness, is not therefore kind; perhaps prosperity becalm'd his breast, perhaps the wind just shifted from the east: Not therefore humble he who seeks retreat, Pride guides his steps and bids him shun the great: who combats bravely is not therefore brave, he dreads death bed like the meanest slave: Who reasons wisely is not therefore wise, His pride in Reas'ning, not in Acting lies.

(Pope)

c. O Friend! I know not which way I must look For comfort, being, as I am, opprest to think that now our life is only drest. For show; mean handiwork of craftsmen, cook, or groom! - We must run glittering like a brook. In the open sunshine, or we are unblest; The wealthiest man among us is the best. No grandeur now in Nature or in book. Delights us. Rapine, avarice, expense. This is idolatry; and these we adore; Plain living and high thinking are no more. The homely beauty of the good old cause. Is gone; our peace, our fearful innocence, And pure religion breathing household laws.

(Wordsworth)

CHAPTER XXIII
COMPREHENSION

COMPREHENSION means understanding what is written in the passage. Preparation for comprehension is the same as for precis and paraphrase.

HOW TO ATTEMPT COMPREHENSION

1. Read the passage carefully and find out the theme or topic. Write down the theme of the passage.

2. Read the passage for the second time and find out the attitude of the author to his subject. Write down the author's approach.

3. A third reading is advisable in order to understand every detail of content and of style. Note down the significant points of detail.

4. Consult the dictionary for the meaning of unknown or uncertain words or phrases. If figures of speech are present take note of their importance and force in the context.

METHOD OF ANSWERING QUESTIONS

1. All answers to questions on comprehension must be simple and concise.

2. All answers must be written in complete sentence except the meaning of words if required.

3. All answers should be based on what is said in the comprehension passage. Personal opinion regarding the correctness or otherwise of points in the passage is irrelevant.

EXAMPLE

Read the following passage carefully and answer the questions given.

A traveller whose exclusive purpose is to reach a certain destination in the minimum of time has at once lost half the joy of his journey. He becomes preoccupied with the thought of his goal and this preoccupation makes him intolerant of the fieldly advances of those he meets by the way and blind to the ever changing panorama along his route. He resents delay, finds every inconvenience irksome and frets and fumes at any hitch that threatens to upset his carefully laid plans. There is, it is true, a certain satisfaction in being whirled in comfort through space at breath taking speeds, or in covering long distances carefree in record time. But the satisfaction is purely material and transitory; there is a touch of vain glorious pride about it; and it smacks too much of business. The real, abiding pleasure of travelling lies in the process, not in the accomplishment.

Questions:

1. What possible pleasures are missed by the impatient traveller?

2. What circumstances are likely to make the hasty traveller impatient?

3. What are the writer's views on the pleasures to be derived from mere rapidity and ease of travel?

4. What in simple terms, is the meaning of the last sentence in the passage?

ANSWERS

1. The impatient traveller loses at once half the joy of his journey. He is also unable to enjoy the fieldly advances of those he meets by the way. He is also unable to enjoy the everchanging panorama along his route.

2. Any delay, inconvenience or hitch that threatens to upset his carefully laid plans makes him impatient and resent it.

3. The writer feels that there is surely a kind of pleasure in moving about at top speed in open space. But that pleasure is materialistic and transitory. It is a kind of vainglorious pleasure and business like.

4. The pleasure of travelling consists in the process - that is, how we travel and enjoy the sights and sounds; not in merely reaching the destination blindly and taking pride about it.

EXERCISE

Read the following passages carefully and answer the questions given below:

a. Many critics of our public schools maintain that far more stress is placed upon achievements in athletics than in the academic sphere and in particular complain against games being compulsory. They maintain that it is tyranny to compel boys with no athletic bent to spend hours of misery on a cricket or foot ball field. These should be left to themselves, when they would occupy their time more usefully and enjoyably on some profitable creative hobby. The drawback to this argument lies in the facile assumption that every non - athlete has a profitable hobby. This is not true; even if it were, model engineering or stamp collecting is no substitute for being out in the fresh air exercising the muscles and having contact with other human beings. I would compel all boys to play games, but I would protect them fiercely from the heresy that it was their duty to be good at games.

1. What is the complaint of critics against public schools?

2. Why do they say that boys should not be compelled to play games?

3. What according to them is the alternative for playing games?

4. Which is better-enjoying a hobby or being out in the fresh air? Why?

5. What is the opinion of the author regarding games?

b. The word "adventure" embraces a company of great words, including courage, tenacity, selflessness and faith, but its most potent ingredient cannot be expressed in one word. It is the spirit that urges men to volunteer to undertake hazardous tasks. For adventure implies the readiness and desire to embark on a course of action that entails risk. A young child may display an instinct for adventure by climbing out of his play-pen to explore the mysteries of the nursery, but this kind of adventure is hardly laudable because the child has not yet sufficient reasoning power to realise the potential risk in such an action. As we grow older, however, the spirit of adventure tends to be restrained by caution; the fire is often smothered by reason, which gives warning of impending dangers and coldly counsels safety first. Yet in some men the urge for adventure may be so strong that it overwhelms the primary instinct of self preservation and inspires them to attempt the impossible, to reach out for the unattainable.

Questions:

1. What other words does the word "adventure" embrace?

2. What is adventure's most potent ingredient?

3. Why is the action of the child in climbing out of his play-pen not laudable?

4. What happens as we grow older?

5. What is the effect of the urge for adventure in some men?

CHAPTER XXIV
THE ESSAY

$\mathbf{T}$ HE Essay is a composition in which the writer states his knowledge of and gives his opinions about a certain topic. The essay can be narrative, descriptive, historical, political, religious or critical in which the author's own point of view is indicated.

METHOD FOR ESSAY WRITING

Essay writing can be done in four stages. It is very important that essays should be written strictly according to method. The four stages of essay writing are

1. **Think about the subject** and jot down on paper all the facts or ideas that come to you. For this the title of the essay must be read carefully so that exact scope of the subject and how it is going to be approached or treated may be understood.

2. **Arrange the facts** according to topics in order to prepare an outline for the composition. The facts arranged may group themselves under certain heads. If there are five or six topics each topic can form the subject of a paragraph. The essay will then contain five or six paragraphs. Each paragraph will treat different aspect of the subject.

3. **Write the essay**, paying attention to grammar, punctuation and style. In maintaining the style the following points must be noted without fail.

i. Clarity is the most important and essential part of style. Words, phrases and clauses must be in their proper places and all pronouns must be clear in their reference.

ii. Slang, obsolete and colloquial expressions should not find place in the essay for good and immediate effect.

iii. The essay should not be written in the first person. The subject must be treated impersonally and impersonal expressions should be used to qualify a statement.

4. Revise what you have written

Thorough revision of one's own writing is very important. It is by this kind of revision that the student can detect a number of errors committed by him and which can easily be corrected. But if not detected and corrected, the same errors would considerably detract from the value of his work.

Common mistakes to be avoided

a. The paragraph of the essay must not be numbered.

b. Headings must not be introduced in the body of the essay.

c. Single sentence paragraphs should not find place in the essay. In general each paragraph should contain many sentences.

An essay is not, after all, a collection of disjointed paragraphs. It should be considered as a whole and every paragraph has to contribute to the total effect. The first paragraph should lead on to the second, the second on to the third and so on. In order to effect this strategy the opening and closing sentences of each paragraph must be carefully considered and constructed.

The examples belong to four types.

a. those requiring a certain amount of fact - knowledge.

b. those requiring the writer to explain and amplify a given idea.

c. those involving a discussion.

d. those demanding originality of treatment and excellence of style.

a. **Essays requiring some fact-knowledge.**

"Women famous in History"

This topic may fall into this outline.

i. Women had little opportunity of taking part in public affairs.

ii. Famous queens

iii. Famous women who have been the power behind the throne

iv. Heroines of lower rank

v. More recent examples and conclusion.

b. Essays requiring the explanation and amplification of a given idea

The subject of the essay is a statement, generally a quotation or proverb containing an idea that is accepted in general. This accepted idea has to be explained and illustrated. Examples are: Knowledge is Power , Necessity is the mother of Invention ,Honesty is the best policy etc

"The Child is Father of the Man"

A topic like this may have the following outline for its method of treatment.

   i.   introduction

   ii.   Examples where it seems not to apply

   iii.   Examples where great qualities have appeared from earliest years.

   iv.   The general conclusion is that the statement is true.

c. Essays involving Discussion

Very often subjects for the essay demand the opinion or point of view of the writer. They require a proper discussion and expect the writer to take sides. Topics like co-education etc. require the student to make up his mind in respect of the topic and express the opinion in the last paragraph of the essay.

An attempt of such topic as

"Comfort is the aim of Science"

can be outlined like the following:

i. Science gives us plenty of comforts and necessaries of life.

ii. It supplies us also with luxuries.

iii. It mitigates bodily ills.

iv. Still it is not correct to say that comfort is the aim of science.

d. Essays requiring originality and style

Essay topics like 'Proverbs', 'Music', 'Romance', 'Philosophy', etc. belong to this type. Such subjects cannot be exhausted by any writer of an essay. For some subjects the material may be scanty. Essay topics like these give a wide scope for the expression of the writer's personality. Interest can be created by introducing suitable illustrations from history or literature.

9

EXERCISE

1. Define the word 'essay'.

2. What are the stages of essay writing?

3. What mistakes are to be avoided in writing essays?

4. What types of essays can be written?

5. Attempt essays on the following topics

    a. "Penny wise : Pound foolish"

    b. Nothing succeeds like success

    c. Holiday reading

    d. Public opinion

    e. Man among machines

    f. The value of physical exercise.

    g. Your ideal Garden.

    h. "Look before you leap".

CHAPTER XXV
REPORT WRITING

$\mathbf{A}$ report is a piece of information to some person or a body of individuals not in possession of the full facts of the subject with which it deals. The writer of the report must have a good knowledge of the subject of the report though not an expert himself. He is the person who knows more about the subject than the body or the person to whom he reports.

In companies every member of the executive staff like the secretary, the accountant, office manager and others are expected to submit various reports to the Board of Directors as and when they are required. Therefore it is necessary that each executive should be in a position to present or submit, in proper form, his opinion regarding any matter referred to him.

Report writing has a vast scope. The topics or subjects on which reports could be written are innumerable. But a few guiding principles applicable to the types of reports most frequently in vogue can be given. It is not possible to give hard and fast rules.

LETTER REPORTS

Individual reports, reports by an expert to his client, reports of the employee to the employer usually are in the form of a letter. Proper attention must be bestowed on the order in which the items of the report are to be set out. A haphazard arrangement will not be forceful or attractive. An

119

investigator's report is therefore entirely different from the one being drafted for the company.

Reports of the employees to employers usually concern the internal organization and management of the business. The auditors report will be on the finances, assets and liabilities of the company, profit and loss etc.

REPORTS OF COMMITTEES AND SUB COMMITTEES

Reports of committees and sub committees form another class. For more important occasions such reports are sought. Here a number of persons form the committee to conduct investigations and arrive at conclusions. The report is usually couched in formal and carefully chosen phraseology. Not only that, the report is written in personally. It is usually signed by the members of the committee, by the Chairman or by the Chairman and the Secretary.

The final report explains the terms of reference, the aim of the committees, investigations, the investigations made, the names of witnesses examined with details of evidence given and precis of the discussions after the facts have been ascertained. The decision if arrived at is given usually in the form of a recommendation for the consideration of the person or body to whom the report is addressed.

EXAMPLE

Report on the damage caused by fire

The President,   17th April 1989.
College Committee,
Educational Trust,
Madras - 600 017.

Dear Sir,

I regret to inform you that a fire broke out at the College premises here on the night of 15th April 1989. The fire was discovered in the N.C.C. office by the night watchman at 11.15 p.m. Immediately the Fire Brigade was summoned by telephone and the Brigade were at work within 15 minutes of the discovery of the fire.

The N.C.C. office was gutted completely except for the iron rafters and bars. Efforts were made to save the adjoining buildings and with great difficulty they were saved except for the blistered paint and broken windows.. The other departments are undamaged.

The cause of the fire is unknown and it is assured that the attender in charge of the stores in the N.C.C. office was careless. Further enquiries are being made.

The N.C.C. Directorate to which our College Unit is attached is being informed about the accident. Fortunately the stores section is unaffected by fire.

Though the N.C.C. office is gutted, except for the time taken to clear off the debris, no other inconvenience is caused for either the staff or students or public. The College classes can go on as usual, with the precaution that no student is allowed to come near the N.C.C. office for any reason. The N.C.C. officer of the College is requested to ensure this.

Yours   faithfully,

S.Ramachandran
Secretary

Report to a Director on a serious accident

S.Joseph,E.S.Q.,   8th June, 1980
Jesus Villa
9, Village Road
Nungambakkam
Madras

Dear Sir,

I regret to report that at 10.30 A.M. 6th June the upper part of the east wall and a portion of the roof of the premises of the company's offices and stores at this address collapsed without warning. As a result of this sudden unforeseen accident a stores clerk and a packer in the service of the company were killed.

The collapse was quite unexpected as the building was considered safe. When the contractor's attention was drawn to a crack in the ceiling, during internal redecoration he dismissed it as normal state of affair.

The architect's inspection revealed that some of the beams were decayed and that the walls themselves were not strong enough to stand considerable vibration. As the building is on the main road on which the heavy lorries ply continuously along with the company's own lorries. The building is subjected to constant vibration. This according to the architect is the cause of the accident.

The Managing Director has given instructions for relief operations on a war footing. Every assistance will be given to the relatives of those who have been so unfortunately killed. Notice of a Board Meeting which has been called to confirm his action and decide on the steps to be taken is enclosed.

We are fully insured against any claims that may be made by the dependents of our deceased employees and against any claims that may be made in consequence of the death of our stores clerk.

Immediately after the accident occured I notified the insurance companies of the casualities.

Yours faithfully,

E.Williams
Secretary

EXERCISE

1. Write a Report on damage done by fire or explosion and the means of carrying on business during rebuilding

2. Write a report on the celebration of "National Integration Day" in your College.

3. File a report to the editor of a Newspaper about the bus accident that you saw on the highway.

4. Write a Report on the fall in business and give suggestions for stopping the decline

5. Make a Report on your proposed new business and the locality where you want to set it up.

CHAPTER XXVI
DIALOGUE WRITING

D IALOGUE as opposed to monologue is a conversation or talk between two persons. While monologue or soliloquy is generally called loud thinking and involves only one individual, dialogue requires two people to exchange their ideas. Monologues are used by dramatists to familiarize the audience with the ideas and aspirations of a character generally a hero or villain. We find brilliant and thought provoking monologues or soliloquies in Shakespeare plays particularly in Hamlet, Othello, King Lear, Macbeth, King Richard II and others.

Dialogues, purely literary, have almost become extinct. We find these dialogues in plays and novels of the 19th century or even earlier. The main purpose of the dialogue is to exchange views and the easier it is done the better for the participants.

Dialogues can be of many kinds depending upon the persons concerned. A meeting between two friends may start a dialogue on topics in which they are mutually interested. The top may be general, of their studies, subjects, preferences, ideas. Two politicians can have a discussion through dialogue on the party position, chances in elections and the like. Two philosophers can talk on the relative merits of different systems of philosophy or logic. Scientists can always have a dialogue on the latest trends in inventions and discoveries. Thus historians, poets, journalists and ordinary citizens can have a dialogue on whatever topic they are interested in.

Dialogue writing requires a proper understanding of the language and usage of idioms and phrases and construction of sentences. Otherwise it will be very difficult to take part in the conversation.

A few examples are given below to illustrate the points given above.

Example 1

Dialogue between two friends on the merits and demerits of the cinema.

Ramu : Hello! Govind, Where are you going?

Govind : Hello! Ramu. I am going to the theatre.

Ramu : What is the picture at the theatre?

Govind : It is 'Satya' featuring the popular star Kamalahasan.

Ramu : I heard that the picture is full of violence. Isn't it?

Govind : Yes. But that is according to the story

Ramu : Of late, Govind, modern pictures are full of violence and the theatre resounds with terrible noise and background music.

Govind : You are right. The plot is such.

Ramu : Whatever may be the plot, I feel that too much of violence, fights , murders etc. should not be exhibited on the silver screen.

Govind : What makes you say so?

Ramu : Because the cinema, Radio, T.V. are very powerful media that can do immense good or bad to the younger generation. By attending such pictures quite often the young minds are polluted and they would like to do in real life what the heroes and villains do on the screen. If a good message is given by the producer the same can be absorbed by the young and it will be a great service to the society. But unfortunately the producer wants his money back and takes the public for a ride and mixes all sorts of things in the story - especially violence sex and glamour.

Govind : Oh, I see, Now, I clearly understand why too many pictures are full of sex, violence and glamour. I was under the impression that these things were natural and part of the story, Ramu! Thank you very much for opening my eyes. I will hereafter be very selective in seeing pictures. Anyway, having booked the ticket earlier, I cannot avoid seeing this picture today.

Ramu : Doesn't matter Govind. I am happy that you have realised the main drawback in seeing all sorts of riffraff pictures, good bye.

Govind : Good bye!

Example 2

Dialogue between two students on the role of politics in education

Prasad : Good Morning Prasanth! What are you reading?

Prasanth: Good Morning Prasad! I am reading the daily 'The Hindu'

Prasad : What is the news today? Any thing specially important?

Prasanth: Yes, there is a news item regarding students and politics.

Prasad : I personally feel that students should not dabble in politics. They come to schools and colleges for studies and they should not waste their precious time, money and energy by joining politics.

Prasanth: In a way you are correct. But students are the future legislators and rulers of the country. Should they not train and familiarize themselves with what is happening in the country? It is only when they start early they can reach their goal.

Prasad : I agree with you. I do not say that students should not read politics. They must first qualify themselves by reading very well and getting their degrees or diplomas. A student has no other avocation but studies. Nothing should interfere with his studies as long as he is a student. While reading properly a student can keep himself abreast of what is happening in his town, district, state, country and in the world. There is no harm in it. But taking active part in politics and thereby spoiling his education, is a wrong step.

Prasanth: What about the pre-independent days when a number of young men and women jumped into politics leaving their studies and profession? Did they not become great politicians?

Prasad : Yes, absolutely correct. Those days were different. It was necessary for Indians to unite and fight the British for achieving political independence. The situation is totally different now. First of all India requires good citizens, doctors, engineers, lawyers, technicians, scientists, etc.

Prasanth: Now I see your point. I do feel that students, though interested in politics should never take active part in politics and spoil their education. Once they complete their studies with credit they may chalkout their own course in life whether it is politics or some other field.

Prasad : It is time now for my break fast. Let me take leave of you Prasanth. We had a nice exchange of views. Bye!.

Example 3

Dialogue between two friends on the value of sports

Raghu : Good Morning Madhu! Sorry I couldn't attend the prize distribution yesterday.

Madhu : Good Morning! Doesn't matter. See the prizes now. This is the Athletic Championship Cup. This is the I prize in High Jump, this medal for 200 mts race, this one for pole vault.

Raghu : Excellent! How happy I am to see all these prizes! Congratulations. Some how I am not interested in games and sports. I like to read more and become a scholar.

Madhu : That is good, of course. But you know the proverb 'A sound mind in a sound body! Unless you maintain good health your mind will not be healthy. You must not be a bookworm.

Raghu : I feel that by playing games I will not be able to study well.

Madhu : Not at all. By playing games you develop good personality. You will be healthy. You can devote more time for studies. Work while you work play while you play is the saying. Evenings must be devoted to playing, exercise and relieve the boredom out,of attending classes from the morning. I am an average student but a good sports man.

Raghu : Yes, I am a very good student but a very poor sportsman. I will surely start playing games at least from now onwards. Thank you for your suggestion.

CHAPTER XXVII
PARAGRAPH WRITING

LONG passages of Prose are divided into paragraphs. A paragraph is a group of sentences which aim at expressing a single idea. The construction of a paragraph is akin to that of a sentence.

Unity is the most important quality of a paragraph. Every sentence in a paragraph must have a definite relation to the main topic. Even if a single sentence in the paragraph does not conform to this principle, the paragraph becomes faulty. The theme of a well constructed paragraph can as well be expressed in a single sentence.

In a paragraph, the sentence, that indicates the theme is called the topic sentence.

The topic sentence may be at the beginning or at the end of the paragraph depending on the effect the writer wants to create. The topic sentence, generally is found at the beginning in order to arrest the attention of the reader. Thus he may understand immediately the main idea of the paragraph. The placement of the topic sentence at the end of the paragraph reduces the chances of its being recognised and understood.

PARAGRAPHS WITH TOPIC SENTENCES
Examples

When I was a boy almost every one wore boots Some were buttoned and some were laced, and I remember a great

131

aunt who wore the elastic sided variety. Men wore the kind with a row of studs at the top round which to twist the lace and a loop at the back with which to tug them on to the feet in the hurried minutes after breakfast.

The above paragraph starts with a general statement and the following sentences expand the idea of every one by referring in detail to men, women and girls, boys and children.

Another extremely important quality of a paragraph is its **Coherence.** There should be logic in the order of sentences and the transition from one sentence to another should be smooth and easy. There must be clarity in the sequence of thought. The connectives like 'however' 'moreover', 'again', 'on the other hand' 'above all' and 'in conclusion' should be used judiciously. This quality of coherence is absolutely necessary in long paragraphs.

In some paragraphs the topic sentence may not be detected but the theme is always distinct and can be easily stated in a single sentence.

Emphasis is another quality necessary for the construction of a paragraph. The most important part of the paragraph, the topic sentence should be emphasized and its placement in the beginning of the paragraph looked in to. Repetition can also be effectively used in writing a paragraph but it needs careful manipulation.

There is no hard and fast rule for the length of the paragraph. Ideas can be put in a small paragraph of six or twelve lines. Some other ideas require half a page or even more for proper expression. It is always better to write paragraphs of medium length - not very short, not very long.

EXPANSION OF AN IDEA INTO A PARAGRAPH

Usually in this type of expansion the topic sentence is given and the student has to expand the main idea into a decent paragraph. The rules given in earlier pages will show him the method of writing the paragraph.

Example

Expand the following idea into a well constructed paragraph

a. **A man is known by the company he keeps**

We say generally 'Birds of the same feather flock together'. People and personalities with similar ideas, hopes, fears, desires, attitudes and aspirations meet and develop close contact. They become friends and nurture their friendship. For example a politician will make friends with another politician, a student with another student, a businessman with another businessman and so on. So friendship and the company one keeps reveals the nature of the person. Another saying points out, Tell me your friends, I will tell you what you are Keeping company with high dignitaries, politicians, great scholars, scientists, musicians and others who have achieved distinction in their fields is always an asset. It speaks of a person's identity of views and ideas with them in one way or other. On the other hand if one keeps low company it speaks ill of him because of the baser values that inspire his friends. So associations are very powerful and reveal the nature of persons without opening the mouths and speaking.

b. **The luxury of yesterday is the necessity of today.**

In olden days people led a contented life without sophistication. Their desires were few and far between. They were simple and contented men. But scientific advancements, inventions have revolutionised society. Man today has endless needs and necessities. Once a bicycle was a luxury. People used to walk for miles together. But today the situation is different. We have the moped, scooter, motorbike, car - various brands in each vyeing with one another. All these modes of transport which people could n't even dream of yesterday have become the terrible necessities of life today. A person who has no bike or scooter or another vehicle is simply looked down upon. Televisions have become common place in ordinary households where radio was a great luxury once. Washing machines, Vacuum cleaners, mixies, grinders, refrigerators, fans etc. - very costly items have become the order of the day. The family man's needs have increased infinitely and science has whetted his appetite for new things that give him convenience.

c. **Money may not make a person happy, but it is better to be unhappy with money than without it.**

Happiness is a quality of the mind. It is also relative. We cannot define happiness absolutely. Money makes many happy for the simple reason that they have plenty of it. Accumulation of money or wealth has its own dangers. Sons become enemies, wives and relations await the death of a moneyed man to get at his wealth. Wealth tax, Income tax and other payments irk the capitalist. Above all money and material amassed can be easily stolen. All these possibilities make the man very unhappy. By luxurious living the rich man may spoil his health and inspite of his means he may be kept on diet and feel the pangs of desire unfulfilled. Money cannot buy happiness as consumer goods are bought. But still money has its own advantages. Poverty is the worst thing that a man can suffer from. Between the two it is better to be unhappy with money than without it. Without money nothing can be done. Man has no value without money. That is why poor people suffer for want of food, clothing, shelter and all other necessities of life. The rich have everything but they also suffer on account of ill health and other difficulties arising out of too much of money.

CHAPTER XXVIII
PRECIS-WRITING

PRECIS is derived from a French word 'Pressee' which means 'Precise' in English. Therefore to write a Precis is to be precise, to be exact. Precis writing is to summarize the given passage. It is a very good but not an easy exercise in composition.

Precis writing aims at giving the gist or summary of the passage in as few words as possible. Brevity is the soul of the precis. A precis should be clear and full in all details which includes all the essential points. Its aim is to give the reader a grasp of all the chief points in the passage and a fair and general effect of the passage.

Often Precis writing is confused with paraphrase. Paraphrase includes not only a summary but all the details in the given poem or passage. In other words it is some times longer than the given passage. But a precis should not be long. It must be always shorter than the original. It must, as stated earlier, be precise, exact, brief, and without the unnecessary details that are generally found in the passage. The most important thing for a precis is to give the main theme of the passage only bereft of all needless details and ornaments etc. Generally a precis should be one third of the length of the original passage.

Important steps for precis writing:

1. Read the passage carefully at least twice.

2. Find out by another reading what the passage is all about.

3. Underline the important ideas. Leave out all repetitions and unnecessary things.

4. Write down the main ideas in separate headings and sub headings.

5. At last sum up the matter and supply the title. This makes up the rough draft of the passage.

6. Consider if all the most important ideas have been included logically bringing out the essence of the passage.

7. Give a bold title relevant and particular to the passage.

The presentation of ideas:

1. Maintain a clear, simple and lucid style.

2. As far as possible use your own words. Words and phrases, as a rule, should not be reproduced in the precis unless absolutely essential.

3. Use indirect form of speech only.

4. The precis must be a 'connected whole' ...not Jerky or abrupt.

5. Don't introduce irrelevant ideas.

6. Examples, figure of speech, anecdotes etc. must be avoided.

7. Develop good word power to write a good precis. This helps in contracting a given passage reducing its length considerably.

8. The precis should be written in correct grammatical English.

The most important aspect of precis writing is the art of condensation or compression. The student need not follow the original order of thought in the given passage. It is enough if the meaning is expressed more clearly and concisely. In condensing all repetitions should be omitted along with illustrations and examples. Figures of speech can be changed into literal expressions. Phrases can be compressed to words.

Students may carefully follow the examples given below:

1. His courage in battle might without exaggeration be called lion like .
   He was **very brave** in battle.

2. The account the witness gave of the incident moved everyone that heard it to laughter .
   The witness's story was **absurd**.

3. There came to his recollection .
   He **remembered**.

4. The Clerk who is now in his employ.
   His **present** clerk.

5. They acted in a manner that rendered them liable to prosecution .
   They acted **illegally**.

6. He got up and made a speech on the spur of the moment .
   He spoke **off hand**.

7. John fell into the river and before help could reach him, he sank.
   John was **drowned** in the river.

8. He was hard up for money and was being pressed by his creditor.
   He was in **financial difficulties.**

Compress the following figurative expressions into simple English:

Example: He demanded his **pound of flesh.**

Answer : He demanded his **rights.**

1. The King ignored **the writing on the wall.**
Ans:

2. All her projects proved to be **castles in the air.**
Ans:

3. He rides on the crest of **a wave of popularity.**
Ans:

4. He has to work hard **to keep body and soul together.**
Ans:

5. You cannot **snap your fingers** at public opinion.
Ans

6. **It is in the fitness of things** that a college should honour the memory of its founder.
Ans

7. There **is a probability** that he will come today.
Ans

8. **There can never be two opinions** on the need for economy in public expenditure.

Ans:

9. **There is no knowing** when the man will return.

Ans:

10. **It is difficult to exaggerate the importance of** honesty in public life.

Ans:

Very often a **single word** can be used in the place of a complex verbal phrase, a group of verbs, or even a whole clause.

Example: The robbers **entered the city, butchered the people, looted their property and burnt down the city.**

Answer : The **robbers sacked** the city.

Condense the following sentences by using suitable single words.

1. I had a talk with my uncle and **caused him to start** a night school.

Ans:

2. The simple people **who believe every rumour** that goes round are a source of danger.

Ans:

3. **The writer of this petition, who has chosen to keep back his name**, accuses some high officials of corruption.

Ans:

4. Please **check up the facts and see whether** the statements made here **are true.**

Ans:

5. These people **do not know how** to read or write any language.

Ans:

Clauses of all kinds can be reduced to short phrase if not simple words.

Example: We expect that **you will** be present.
Answer : We expect your **presence.**
    I think that **I will go**
    I think of **going**

Condense the following sentences:

1. The news that you have returned is most welcome.
Ans:

2. The beggar pretended that he was starving.
Ans:

3. John is confident that Tom will win.
Ans:

4. He told me that the college was closed.
Ans:

5. Do you wish that I should go?

Ans:

Adjective and adverbial clauses can also be condensed in the same manner.

Example: The house where his fore fathers lived has been sold.

Answer : His **ancestral house** has been sold.
He could not sleep **because he was afraid of ghosts**.
He could not sleep **for fear of ghosts.**

Condense the following sentences:

1. Tell me the reason why you behaved so strangely.
Ans :

2. I do not know the day when he is to leave.
Ans :

3. I shall show you the house where he resides.
Ans :

4. He entrusts all responsibility to his wife who is a capable woman.
Ans :

5. This man, who cannot sign his own name, has earned a lot of money.
Ans :

Shorten the following sentences:

1. If you had not told me, I should have found the exercise very difficult.
Ans :

2. You may come here or go whenever it pleases you.

Ans :

3. Your argument is so absurd that no one will believe it.

Ans :

4. There was no unemployment while the war was on.

Ans :

5. He was so tall that he could not walk straight.

Ans :

All phrases too can be compressed to single, appropriate words.

Example: Democracy serves **the man in the street**
Answer : Democracy serves the **commoner.** (common man)

Example: His conduct is **deserving of all praise.**
Answer : His conduct is **praise worthy**.

Condense the following sentences:

1. He told me a cock and bull story.

Ans:

2. The long and short of the matter is that he is sent to jail.

Ans:

3. That is a man in a thousand.

Ans:

4. He set to work with hammer and tongs.

Ans:

5. We discussed the pros and cons of the question.

Ans:

Shorten the following sentences:

1. He is a man of popularity.
Ans:

2. He is aware of your defects.
Ans:

3. Visitors to this place are few and far between.
Ans:

4. He stole a pen belonging to my brother.
Ans:

5. His good qualities are too many to list.
Ans:

6. The money lost was in the neighbourhood of a few thousands.
Ans:

7. The rain soaked us through and through.
Ans:

8. I visit my uncle now and then.
Ans:

9. He used to come in every now and then
Ans:

10. The two letters arrived at the same time.
Ans:

Prepositional phrases as well as verbs that have the same subject can be condensed with the help of participal construction.

Example: In the event of your coming we shall take a car. If you come we shall take a car. When he had said his say, he left the room.

Compress the following sentences:

1. With regard to his qualification I know nothing.
Ans:

2. All of a sudden she began to weep.
Ans:

3. By and by he was cured.
Ans:

4. She entered the hall and locked herself in.
Ans:

5. The rain had stopped now and so he went away.
Ans:

Negative particles in sentences can be removed and the sense shifted to the subject or object. By substituting for the verb its opposite, a kind of shortening and economy of words takes place.

Example: He did **not see anything.**
He **saw nothing.**
His draft was **not honoured.**
His draft was **dishonoured.**

145

Shorten the following sentences:

1. People are not permitted to smoke here.

Ans:

2. He is not to be seen anywhere.

Ans:

3. Permission was not given for conducting the meeting.

Ans:

4. They are not unaware of what is happening here.

Ans:

5. He does not obey his brother.

Ans:

Therefore, in a precis, the point to note is the number of words used and not their length.

PRECIS WRITING

EXAMPLE

ORIGINAL

The Greeks saw that they must devise a secret method of entering the city, or they must accept defeat and sail home. The result of this realization was the birth of a grand stratagem in the mind of Odysseus. He got a skilful worker in wood to make an enormous wooden horse which could conceal within its hollow body a number of armed men. His plan was that certain of the chieftains should hide inside it along with himself, while all the other Greeks should strike camp and pretend to sail away. But really they would hide the beyond the nearest island and watch the developments unseen by the Trojans. Odysseus planned to leave behind in the Greek camp a single Greek who would have a ready tale to tell the Trojans and make them draw the huge wooden horse not the city. Once the horse into was inside the walls, the Greeks concealed inside were to leave their wooden prison when the night was at its darkest, open the gates of the city, and let their friends in who by then would have sailed back under cover of darkness and be waiting outside the city walls. Then was to commence an orgy of killing and burning and looting, that was not to cease till the proud city was razed to the ground.   (221)

FIRST DRAFT

The Greeks realized that unless they contrived a secret entry they would never take the city. Odysseus, accordingly, formed a plan. He got an enormous wooden horse made, inside which would lie concealed armed Greeks including himself. The Greeks would pretend to sail away, but return under cover of night. A solitary Greek staying behind would, with a lying tongue, persuade the Trojans to drag the horse to the city. In the night, the concealed warriors would slip out and open the gates. Their waiting friends would rush in and start an orgy of killing and burning that would destroy the city.   (102)

Obviously, further condensation is necessary. Underline the words that is capable of further compression and make another attempt.

FINAL PRECIS

THE STRATAGEM OF THE
WOODEN HORSE

Realizing the impossibility of taking Tröy except by stratagem, Odysseus got an enormous wooden horse made within which to conceal armed chieftains including himself. The others striking camp would seemingly depart, but return unnoticed after nightfall. Persuaded by a cunning Greek, the Trojans would drag the wooden horse into their city where that night the concealed Greeks would steal out and open the gates for the Greek hosts to enter and sack the city.

Make a precis of the following:

Our mechanical civilization has in no way made man better than he was a few hundred years ago. Compared with the African native our factory workman is dull and helpless. The negro is sprightly and self-supporting. He is generally well-informed regarding the phenomena of nature and the habits of birds and beasts. He has his traditional religion, his myths and his folklore. He is handy and helpful. He can build his house, obtain and prepare his food, make a fire without matches, spin his yarn, weave his cloth and make and handle his tools. Physically he is robust and energetic and even humorous.

On the other hand we have developed our factory workman on one side only. We have made him a slave of labour, without creating in him the least interest in what he produces. He often does not know what he is doing mechanically. Our factory hand is not a manufacturer. He has no inventive power, no individual craftsmanship. He has little skill and no ambition. He has little knowledge and less culture. He works hard in unwholesome conditions and he is housed, fed and clothed miserably. It is not his fault, for he is made to live a truly mechanized life, without being taught the art of living.

Make a precis of the following:

One of the drawbacks observed in our schools is that even village children (and much more town-bred ones) are unused and unwilling to handle the broom, the duster, the water pot or the shovel. All these instruments are duly wielded by the children in a Montessori school, where there are no servants but all the work of cleaning and tidying is done with joy and pride by all the children individually and in groups. In the atmosphere of activity which pervades the whole school there is no distinction between high and low work - there is no room for our millennial caste-mind. Everyone works and no one is superior or inferior. Madame Montessori had never heard of our 'socialistic pattern of society' (whatever it may mean) when she made children so early in life forget distinctions and divisions which are our speciality. Would India not profit by such training of her children at the very start of their existence?   (158)

Attempt a precis of the following passage :

Thousands and thousands of books are bought every year, every month, every day by people who do not read at all. They only think that they read. They buy books just to amuse themselves, 'to kill time' as they call it' in one hour or two their eyes have passed over all the pages and there is left in their minds a vague idea or two about what they have been looking at and this, they really belive, is reading. Out of a thousand persons who say 'I have read this' or ' I have read that' there is not perhaps one who is able to express any opinion worth hearing about what he has been reading. Many and many a time I hear students say that they have read certain books; but if I ask them questions regarding the book, I find that they are not able to make any answer or at best, they will only repeat something that somebody else has said about what they think they have been reading. But this is not peculiar to the students; it is in all countries the way that the great public devour book. I would say that the difference between the great critic and the common person is chiefly that the great critic knows how to read, and that the common person does not. No man is really able to read a book who is not able to express an original opinion regarding the contents of a book. The first thing a scholar should bear in mind is that a book ought not to be read for mere amusement. Half-educated persons read for amusement and are not to be blamed for it. But a young man who has passed through a course of university training should discipline himself at an early date never to read for mere amusement. He will then throw down any book from which he cannot obtain intellectual food, any book which does not make an appeal to the higher emotions and to his intellect.

Write a precis of the following passage:

Our generation in its rapid travel has not achieved the habit of reading great books and has the habit of being influenced by the great classics of our country. If the principles of democracy in our Constitution are to become habits of mind and pattern of behaviour, principles which change the very character of the individual and the nature of society, it can be done only by the study of great literature, of philosophy and religion. That is why even though our country needs great scientists, great technologists, great engineers, we should not neglect to make them humanists. No university can regard itself as a true university unless it sends out young men and women who are not only learned but whose hearts are full of compassion for suffering humanity. Unless that is there, university education must be regarded as incomplete.

It hurts me very deeply when I find that the precious years during which a student has to live in the university are wasted by some of them. Teachers and students form a family and in a family you cannot have the spirit of the trade union. Such a thing should be inconceivable in a university. University life is a co-operative enterprise between teachers and students and I do hope that the students will not do a disservice to themselves by resorting to activities which are anti-social in character.

Character is that on which the destiny of a nation is built. One cannot have a great nation with men of small character. Whether in public life or student life, we cannot reach great heights if we are lacking in character. We cannot climb the mountain when the very ground at our feet is crumbling. When the very basis of our structure is shaky, how can we reach the heights which we have set before ourselves?

Epitomize the following passage, reducing it to about One third of its length

The joys of freedom are indeed difficult to describe; they can only be fully appreciated by those who have had the misfortune to lose them for a time. With grief and sorrow I occasionally notice that here and there are people who speak of freedom as though it were a mechanical invention, or the quick specific for which they have taken up a patent. Our ancestors', say they, 'have fought, have sacrificed and have suffered for freedom. It is ours exclusively. We will not share it with those who have not shared our antecedent troubles, trials and misfortunes to attain it. Come, take it if you can, but give it we will not. I take it that this is not an exalte view of freedom. Humanity would be but a poor witness to the wisdom of the All Wise, if the experience through which it has gone were to yield benefit only to those who have gone through it. History would be a dead thing, all our trails and misfortunes would be superfluous, if we compelled posterity in its turn to go through similar ordeals. What a man has fought for and won, he must without reserve or qualification share with his fellowmen. Sanitarians preach that you can never enjoy the best health in your house till your surroundings are also well developed in the matter of hygiene. Philosophers tell us that you can best seek your own happiness only by serving for the happiness of others; So I believe no man will enjoy to the fullest measure the blessings of freedom unless he shares them to the full with his fellowmen.

Write a precis of the following passage:

One day Marya was in the room when Bronya was having a reading lesson with her mother and father. Bronya was not a stupid child, but at seven years old she was not much interested in reading. She stumbled over the words of her reading-book. Suddenly little Marya took the book out of her hands and read the first sentence without a mistake. When she looked up excitedly from the book, her mother and father gazed each other in silent astonishment. They were afraid that their baby was going to be precocious and conceited. Bronya, too, instead of being proud of her pupil, was looking at her with a sulky stare on her fair dimpled face. Poor Marya began to cry, 'Pardon, pardon', she sobbed, I didn't do it on purpose. It's not my fault, it's not Bronya's fault. It's only because it was so easy.

Between the time when she learnt to read and the day when, as Mme Marie Curie she became a member of the French Academy of Medicine, Marya Skoldovska's life was full of sadness, but also of wonderful adventure. Until the year 1918, her country, Poland did not regain its independence. It had been partitioned three times by the end of the eighteenth century and Warsaw, where her parents lived, was ruled by the Czar of Russia. Her father was a schoolmaster, but he was not free to teach as he liked. In one wing of the school lived a Russian inspector who would report him if he taught his boys to love their country or to use their own Polish language.

When Marya was ten years old she herself went to school. Her class teacher was a Pole, and taught the children Polish history in Polish. If a bell in the corridor warned them that an inspector had come, the Polish Books had quickly to be cleared and Marya, as the surest child in the class, would be chosen to answer questions about Russia to give the titles of Czar and names of the Imperial family.

Without a single mistake she played her part but when the inspector had gone and her teacher kissed her, she bursts into tears. Two years later her father was turned out of his house in the school buildings and had to move with his delicate wife and his son and little daughters from their pleasant home into a much smaller house. He had less money and had to take school boys to board with him. The little girls had to sleep and work in the dining room. Soon their mother died and they were left to the care of a house-keeper and of their father in such time as he could spare from his work.

Write a precis of the following passage:

After six months thus spent in Ahmedabad, we started for England. In an unlucky moment I began to write letters about my journey to my relatives and to the Bharati. Now it is beyond my power to call them back. These were nothing but the outcome of useful bravado. At that age the mind refuses to admit that its greatest pride is in its power to understand, to accept, to respect; and that modesty is the best means of enlarging its domain. Admiration and praise is looked upon as a sign of weakness or surrender, and the desire to cry down and hurt and demolish with argument gives rise to this kind of intellectual fire works. These attempts of mine to establish my superiority by revilement might have occasioned my amusement today, had not their want of straightness and common courtesy been too painful.

From my earliest year I had practically no commerce with the outside world. To be plunged in this state, at the age of seventeen, into the midst of the social sea of England would have justified considerable misgiving as to my being able to keep afloat. But as my sister-in-law happened to be in Brighton with her children I weathered the first shock of it under her shelter.

Write a precis of the following passage:

The big change I noticed was the increased interest in politics. You cannot understand the modern Indians unless you realise that politics occupy them passionately and constantly, that artistic problems and even social problems-yes and even economic problems-are subsidiary. Their attitude is 'first we must find the correct political solution and then we can deal with the other matters'. I think the attitude is unsound and used to say so; still, there it.is, and they hold it much more vehemently than they did a quarter of a century ago. When I spoke about the necessity of form in literature and the importance of the individual vision, their attention wandered although they listened politely. Literature, in their view, should expound or inspire a political creed.

Externally the place has not changed. It looks much as it did from the train. Outside the carriage windows (rather the dirty windows) it unrolls as before-monotonous, enigmatic and at moments sinister. And in some long motor drives which I took through the Deccan there were the same combinations of hill, rock, bushes, ruins, dusty people and occasional yellow flowers which I encountered when I walked on the soil in my youth. There is still poverty, and since I am older today and more thoughtful, it is the poverty. The malnutrition which persists like a ground swell beneath the pleasant froth of my immediate experience. But I do know that people ought not to be so poor and to look so ill, and that rates ought not to run about them as I saw them doing in a labour camp at Bombay. Industrialism has increased, though it does not dominate the landscape yet, as it does in the west. You can see the chimneys of the cotton mills at Ahmedabad, but you can see its mosques too; you can see little factories near Calcutta, but they are tucked away amongst bananas and palms, and the one I have in mind has an enormous tree overhanging it in whose branches a witch is said to sit, and from whose branches huge fruit occasionally fall and hit the corrugated iron roofs with a bang, so that the factory hands jump. No.......externally India has not changed

Write a precis of the following passage:

The aim of education is that the pupil should acquire an automatic appreciation of values, moral and other. We do not desire to produce indoctrinated minds. That is not the democratic ideal. Totalitarians may wish to give a twist in a planned direction while the mind is young but our aim should be to produce a free and faithful intellectual and moral apparatus, rather than to give pre-arranged twist.

Again, it should be remembered that which is compulsory automatically induces distaste. If you wish boys and girls to develop a permanent and unreasoning dislike of anything, make that subject compulsory. If you wish that they may develop a willingness and a capacity to appreciate good literature such as the Ramayana and the Mahabharata, or Shakespeare, or the Bible, for God's sake, I would say to the educationists, do not make the study of the Ramayana and the Mahabharata or of Shakespeare or the Bible, compulsory in the school. The lessons of both child psychology and human psychology are that mandatory and compulsory direction produces a contrary and rebellious tendency. The conditions for assimilation should be produced, and there should be no compulsion. Youth should be produced and there should be no compulsion. Youth should be helped, to choose good things for itself rather than be forced and drilled.

Therefore I would suggest to educationists that less stress should be laid on examinations and more on opportunities for study and assimilation. The examination is the most bitter part of compulsion. It creates an incurable tendency towards superficiality and a paradoxical condition wherein a certain degree of equipment and dislike go together. Once the examination is over, it leaves in the successful candidate a distaste for further advance.

Write a precis of the following passage:

In this world of incessant and feverish activity, men have little time to think much less to consider ideals and objectives. Yet, how are we to act even in the present unless we know which way we are going and what our objectives are? It is only in the peaceful atmosphere of a University that these basic problems can be adequately considered. It is only when the young men and women who are in the University today and on whom the burden of life's problems will fall tomorrow, learn to have clear objectives and values that there is hope for the next generation.

The past generation produced some greatmen, but as a generation it led the world repeatedly to disaster. Two World Wars are the price that has been paid for the lack of wisdom on man's part in this generation. It is a terrible price and an even deeper tragedy is that mankind does not profit by its experience and continues to go the same way which led previously to disaster.

We have had wars and we have had victory and we have celebrated that victory, yet what is victory and how do we measure it? A war is fought presumably to gain certain objectives. The defeat of the enemy is not by itself an objective but rather the removal or an obstruction towards the attainments of the objective. If that objective is not attained, then that victory over the enemy brings only negative relief and indeed is no real victory. We have seen however, that the aim in wars is almost entirely to defeat the enemy and the other and real objective is often forgotten. Therefore, it becomes necessary to have the real objectives clear in our minds at all times, whether in war or in peace and always aim to achieve that objective.

CHAPTER XXIX
LETTER WRITING

L ETTER writing is an art in itself. But the literary letter as written by John keats and others has died down. A letter is, to all intents and purposes, an intimate personal conversation between persons beyond reach of conversation. The hall mark of a good and great letter is its simplicity, lucidity and personal or subjective touch.

In business and official letters the writer should conform to the accepted standards while in private letters to friends and relatives he may be free and informal. All letters generally should indicate the name and address of the addressee, the date of despatch, and the writer's signature at the end of the letter in its appropriate place. Letters are expected to be polite brief, and clear in diction and highly informative.

Various kinds of letters are in Vogue:

1. Business letters (between the supplier and customer).

2. Letters between merchants of different status in business.

3. Official letters between equals and the higher bosses.

4. Applications for Jobs, donations etc.

5. Letters seeking or giving various types of information.

6. Social letters like invitations etc.

7. Private and personal letters between family members and friends.

159

All these letters can be broadly grouped into two main division. They are

1. Formal Letters (Business Letters)
2. Informal Letters (Personal Letters)

INFORMAL OR PERSONAL LETTERS

An informal letter has the following parts or divisions in addition to the address on the envelope.

1. The address of the writer.

2. The date

3. The salutation or greeting

4. The body of the letter.

5. The subscription or proper closing

6. The signature

THE FORMAT OF AN INFORMAL LETTER

```
                                1. The address of the writer
                                2. Date

  3.  The salutation
  4.  The body of the letter


                                5. The subscription
                                6. The signature
```

1. Write the address on the top right hand corner of the page or letter.
   Every line should have a comma at the end.
   Put a full stop at the end of the last line.

New form	**Old form**
14 Raghavachari Street,	14 Raghavachari Street
Perambur,	Perambur
Madras-11.	Madras-11.

2. Write the date at the end of the sender's address:

> 14, Raghavachari Street,
> Perambur,
> Madras-11.

19.8.87 or 19th August, 1987 or August 19, 1987. Put a full stop after writing the date.

3. The Salutation depends on the relationship the writer has to the person to whom he is writing a letter.

   a. Address your friend by his/her name only

   e.g. Dear Ramu, Gopal, Sheela, Asha etc.
   Don't address as 'Dear friend'

   b. Address parents or relatives as : Dear father, mother, grandfather, grandmother, uncle, aunt, brother, sister etc.

   Salutation must be to the left hand side of the letter on the next line after the date. Put a comma after the salutation.

4. **The body of the letter**: This is the most important part of the letter. The language should be simple and lucid. The letter should be intensely personal as if you are speaking to a person.

5. **The subscription**: The letter ends with the subscription or complimentary close at the right side of the page. The commonest form of closing a letter to parents and relatives is.

> Yours affectionately,
> Your loving son/daughter.

To a friend : Yours sincerely,
Ever sincerely yours,
Your sincere friend,

Put a comma after subscription. Note that there is no apostrophe in, Yours.

6. **The Signature**: The place of signature is below the subscription and more to the right as in:

> Yours faithfully,

At the centre towards the lower half of the envelope should be written the address of the person to whom the letter is sent. The name first is followed by his address and pincode number. The words 'Mr.' 'Mrs.' and 'Miss' can be used before the names.

FORMAL OR BUSINESS LETTER

A business or formal letter is different from the personal or informal letter. It has clearly two differences. The first difference is in its form and the second in its language.

A formal or business letter is written for a specific purpose. The motive of the writer is to transact some business. The essence of a formal letter, therefore, is its precise nature and writing to the point.

A business or formal letter has the following parts of divisions.

1. Sender's address
2. The Date
3. The Inside address
4. The Salutation
5. The body of the letter
6. The Subscription
7. The Signature

1. **The Sender's address** is the same as in the informal or personal letter.

2. **The Date** is in the same position as in the personal letter below the sender's address.

3. **The Inside address** is on the left side of the letter, two or three lines below the line of the date.

Example:

Sender's address
Date:

To

The Director,
Institute of Correspondence Education,
Chepauk,
Madras - 600 005.

4. Salutation should be written below the next line after the side address is written.

    e.g.:   The Director,
            Institute of Correspondence Education,
            University of Madras,
            Chepauk,
            Madras - 600 005.

Sir/Madam

If the person is known you may write Dear Mr.Prakasam, or Dear Mrs.Lakshmi

5. **The body of the letter**: There is a lot of difference in the body of the letter (business or formal letter) when compared to that in the personal or informal letter.

Always be clear in your letter, to the point and polite. Cut short all unwanted and unnecessary details. The letter must be complete in all respects with the required information.

6. **The Subscription**:

The usual form is   Yours faithfully, or
                                           Yours truly,

In case the salutation has a personal name the subscription should be

                                           Yours sincerely,

7. **The Signature**: Sign your name in full in a formal letter. Put the date below the signature. Below that write the name of the sender in brackets in capital

letters. If needed, the position of the sender can be written.

e.g.:   Yours faithfully,

                                  (RAMAKRISHNAN)
                                    MANAGER

MODEL LETTERS

1.   LETTER OF APPLICATION

                          16,Kandapillai Street,
                          Perambur,
                          Madras-11
                          5th August, 1987.

To

Messrs.Mahendranath & Sons,
Exporters and Importers,
First Line Beach,
George Town,
Madras-600 001.

Gentlemen,

I wish to apply for the post of Junior Clerk, advertised in today's 'The Hindu'.

I am eighteen years young and have just passed the Higher Secondary School Certificate examination from the Pachaiyappa's Higher Secondary School, Madras-1. I have also taken a course in typewriting and shorthand and book-keeping. I have secured a I class in English Typewriting (Higher) and a II class in Shorthand (Lower).

I enclose my testimonials for your reference. You may kindly refer to the headmaster of Pachaiyappa's Higher Secondary School for my Conduct and Character.

If I am given the post, I can assure you I will do my best to give you satisfaction.

Yours faithfully,
N.Rajendran

2. LETTER PLACING AN ORDER FOR GOODS

Ahalya Apartments,
Plot No.24A,
G.N.Chetty Street,
T.Nagar,
Madras-600 017.

The Sales Manager,   July 15, 1992.
Ganesh Publishing House,
18, Conran Smith Road,
Mount Road,
Madras-600 002.

Sir,

Thank you for your letter dated 25th June 1992 and the catalogues. We have gone through the catalogues carefully and wish to place an order for the following books in different disciplines as given below:

1. A Text Book of Geometry edited by   100   Copies
   K.R.S.Menon

2. St.Joan by Bernard Shaw   25   Copies

3. English Prose Selections by Sarup Singh	50	Copies
4. Wuthering Heights by Emily Bronte	50	Copies
5. A Tale of Two Cities by Charles Dickens	50	Copies
6. Silas Marner by George Eliot	100	Copies

Please send the books by T.V.S. Transport to the above address.

We shall bear the transport charges. The books are required urgently and should reach us by 25th July 1992.

We shall remit the amount of the invoice on receipt of the goods. Payment will be made by cheque (Payee's Account) only.

Please note that the right to reject defective material is reserved by us.

Yours faithfully,
(K.S.SIVARAMAKRISHNAN)
Librarian
Brilliant Arts College, Madras.

3. LETTER TO THE EDITOR OF A NEWSPAPER

a. Letters to Newspapers should be addressed to the Editor.

b. The letters end with the subscription, yours truly.

c. The correct form of salutation is Sir, and not Dear Sir.

d. If the writer wants his address to be published, it is to be given below the letter and to the left of the signature.

e. If the writer does not want his name to be published he can sign his letter, with words like 'Interested', 'Anxious', 'Indignant' etc.

To

The Editor,
The Hindu,
Mount Road,
Madras-2.

Sir,

Our Municipality is sleeping over the issue of Water supply in the New Town area. There has been no response or reaction from the Municipality for all the private and public appeals. Perhaps a little publicity through your paper will do no harm. For the past one month the water supply through the Municipal tap has been highly erratic, irregular and scarce. Nearly 20,000 people reside in New Town and it is a sad plight to see ladies and gents carrying empty pots to bring water from wells daily. The Municipality should regulate water supply to various parts of the town. It is this failure on the part of the Municipality that is responsible for the difficulties of people in New Town, Vaniyambadi. It is hoped that the Municipality will, at least, wake up now and do its duty to society and the public immediately.

15.7.1984   Yours truly,
                                                         Indignant

4. LETTER TO POLICE INSPECTOR REQUESTING PROPER ARRANGEMENTS AND BANDOBUST

18,Pillaiyar Koil Street,
Amburpet,
Vaniyambadi.
December 9, 1986.

To

The Inspector of Police,
Town Police Station,
Vaniyambadi, N.A.

Dear Sir,

I would like to draw your kind attention to the fact that thefts have increased in Vaniyambadi since a month. Between October and November nearly 20 houses have been burgled in our town and valuable property lost. In my own locality a neighbour of mine has lost Rs.10,000/- in cash and 20 sovereigns of gold while he was away in Andhra.

I request you to increase the night beats and make necessary bandobust arrangements to check these thefts and create a sense of security among people.

I hope you will do the needful in this connection to remove the sense of fear in the local population.

Yours truly,

S.Venkataraman

MODEL LETTERS
Informal Letters

1. **Letter to Parents & Relations** (about continuing studies further)

> 10, Jamalia Street,
> Saidapet,
> Madras,
> May 7, 1984.

Dear father,

I am very happy to see your letter. In about a week my final year examinations start. I am preparing well for the various papers. I am confident that with the guidance of the teachers and my own personal effort I will surely get a first class in all subjects. You need not worry yourself about my examinations.

After I pass my B.Sc. Examination I want to continue. I would like to do M.Sc., in Chemistry and therefore I want you to be ready to put me in an institution where the course is offered. An ordinary degree of any kind is absolutely of no use in the present context. Therefore I have take this decision and trust that you agree with me and fulfill my desire.

My respects and love to you, mother, brothers and sisters.

> Yours affectionately,
>
> K.N.Sukumar.

To
Shri Raj Mohan, B.A.,
15 Lala Street,
Katpadi Extension,
Vellore-6.

2. LETTER TO A FRIEND: (Sending a gift on his birthday)

5 Krishna Road,
Nungambakkam,
Madras.

6th July 1986

Dear Ramesh,

I am very happy to receive your letter. My hearty congratulations on your 18th birthday. May god in His infinite
Mercy shower on you all the best in life. How I wish I were
present for the occasion.

I had send by Registered Post today a beautiful pen set
as my present for your birthday. Please accept it as a token
of my intimate friendship with you.

I will make it convenient to visit you as early as possible.
I shall remember how much I owe to you for the invaluable
help you rendered to me when you were here with me.

With best wishes.

Yours sincerely,

(P.S.Nathan)

To

S.Ramesh,
S/o.K.S.Narasimhan,
1,Anbu Naiken Street,
Vijayalakshmipurarn,
Ambattur,
Madras-53.

EXERCISE

1. Write a letter to the Director of Education, applying for appointment as a teacher in the Educational Service.

2. Write a letter to the Commissioner of Police, applying for a licence to carry arms, stating reasons.

3. Write a letter to a Newspaper protesting against Street Noises.

4. Write a letter to a Newspaper on reckless driving and accidents.

5. Write a letter to your father asking for permission and money to join the Picnic party in your college. Describe the places you propose to visit and their importance.

6. Write a letter to your principal asking him to send your conduct certificate and T.C.

7. Write a letter to your sister asking her to read well and pass creditably in her 10th Std. Examination.

8. Write a letter to your friend advising him not to join politics and warning him of the bad consequences.

9. Write a letter to a publishing company ordering for various books you require.

10. Draft a letter to a company ordering items of furniture you require for your office.